Primary Schools and Special Needs: Policy, Planning and Provision

Second edition

Sheila Wolfendale

CASSELL

Cassell Educational Limited
Villiers House
41/47 Strand
London WC2N 5JE

387 Park Avenue South
New York, NY 10016–8810
USA

First edition 1987
Second edition first published 1992

British Library Cataloguing-in-Publication Data

A catalogue record for this book is available from the British Library.

Library of Congress Cataloging-in-Publication Data

Wolfendale, Sheila, 1939–
    Primary schools and special needs : policy, planning, and
provision / Sheila Wolfendale.—2nd ed.
        p.   cm.—(Special needs in ordinary schools)
    Includes bibliographical references and index.
    1. Special education—Great Britain.   2. Mainstreaming in
education—Great Britain.   3. Elementary schools—Great Britain—
Curricula.   I. Title.   II. Series.
LC3986.G7W65   1992
371.9′0472′0941—dc20   91–39853
                                                              CIP

ISBN 0–304–32638–0 (hardback)
     0–304–32426–4 (paperback)

FRONT COVER PHOTOGRAPHY BY JOHN WALMSLEY USING MODELS

Typeset by Colset Private Limited, Singapore
Printed and bound in Great Britain by Biddles Ltd, Guildford and King's Lynn

Contents

Editorial foreword

When the first edition of this book was being prepared in 1986, few would have predicted that education in general and primary education in particular were about to be subjected to the most far-reaching changes seen in British schools since 1944, and perhaps even since 1870. Six years later, we need to ask whether these changes will benefit all children, whether they will make for an increasing number of effective and inclusive schools catering for the whole range of personal and individual needs of all children and, specifically, whether schools will be more able to reach out to help those children who for any reason are experiencing difficulties in learning. This book should help readers to come to their own conclusions on this matter by relating their experiences to the national overview of issues presented here.

This series of books was based on the assumption that the curriculum of schools needed to be accessible to all pupils. Since the first edition of this book was published, five years ago, the curriculum of primary schools has begun to be transformed by the introduction of nine distinct subjects, by a plethora of new cross-curricular themes, skills and dimensions, and by the introduction of National Curriculum assessment and records of achievement. The introduction of local management of schools, the undermining of the role of the local education authority and the inducements to schools to opt for grant-maintained status have all contributed to a feeling of innovation overload which is unlikely to be in the interests of vulnerable children.

There is wide agreement that the advent of the National Curriculum has helped all schools to rethink their curriculum and has provided, for the first time, a single common language for teachers from all sectors of education. But even before the Education Reform Act, schools were beginning to re-examine their curriculum in order to make it more accessible to all pupils, including those from ethnic minorities or those whose first language was other than English, as well as pupils with special educational needs.

But there has been a price to pay. The work of primary schools has been subjected to intense publicity and a great deal of misrepresentation. Everything and everyone have been blamed for the apparent decline in reading standards: the National Curriculum, the introduction of national testing, 'real books', the Plowden Report and, of course, teacher trainers preaching 'barmy theories'.

The evaluation of the Leeds Primary School initiatives and the subsequent national report on primary education (Alexander, Rose and Woodhead, 1991) suggested that children with special educational needs were not being helped as much as they might have been and that teacher underestimation of their abilities was still common. This view appeared to be reinforced by the finding that there was a tendency for teachers to record higher levels of attainment on the Standard Assessment Tasks than on teacher assessment, though there are many possible explanations for this discrepancy. At the same time, these reports raised important questions about the balance between group and individual work, pupil-directed learning and problem-solving, and classroom organisation. These issues, all fundamentally relevant to the teaching of pupils with or without special educational needs, are at the heart of this book.

The fierce debates which have surrounded the first years of the Education Reform Act and the considerable volume of research and professional development in primary education have had the positive effect of focusing on the question of what is an effective school. The evidence suggests that effective schools are staffed by people with high expectations of all pupils, regardless of family or cultural background, schools where all children receive intellectually challenging teaching in a work-centred environment characterised by a high level of teacher-pupil communication and praise, schools where tasks are matched to individual pupils and where there is an effective policy of partnership with parents – all themes thoroughly explored in this book.

By the time the third edition of this book comes to be written, say five years from now, how much progress will have been made towards ensuring that we have effective schools for all children?

Professor Peter Mittler
University of Manchester
May 1992

REFERENCE

Alexander, R., Rose, J. and Woodhead, C. (1992) *Curriculum Organisation and Classroom Practice in Primary Schools: A Discussion Paper*. London: DES.

Preface to the second edition

In the five years since this book was first written, there have been cataclysmic changes within education. Fundamental and radical reforms include the introduction of the National Curriculum; mandatory national assessment at four key stages in each child's school life; the source, basis and responsibility for educational funding and spending altered and realigned directly to schools themselves, as well as other minor changes. Special educational needs were evidently not to the forefront of government thinking when the Education Reform Act was initially drafted as a Bill; nevertheless, intensive lobbying by groups, associations of professionals, and parents ensured that certain provisions and safeguards regarding SEN were built into the subsequent Act.

These have since been translated into specific guidelines issued by the National Curriculum Council and the DES for meeting special education needs in mainstream schools and, further, realised into implementation at local level by teachers, advisers, inspectors, educational psychologists and others working with children with special needs.

At the time of preparing this second edition it remains uncertain whether adequate financial and material provision for special needs will be guaranteed in the longer term, and, if so, by what mechanisms. There are a number of major issues to be resolved concerning funding sources, allocation of resources and criteria for eligibility to receive these limited resources.

This book will not speculate on or discuss these issues and their wider implications, though of course they impinge upon its subject matter and so will be referred to in various chapters.

Although there are valid reasons for concern, even anxiety, about ensuring equality of access to educational opportunities, there is at the same time sufficient reason for remaining optimistic that the tremendous amount of good practice that has been and is developing within special needs spheres will continue. This book sets out to record and celebrate these achievements and to align ideas and practices described in the first edition that are still current and demonstrably effective with approaches that have accompanied the advent of the National Curriculum.

The National Curriculum, cornerstone of the 1988 Education Reform Act, pervades these pages. So, too, will other seminal developments that have occurred during the last five years or so and now impinge upon children's lives, or soon will do.

Several of these developments may appear initially to be peripheral to the title of this book, yet the reflective reader will no doubt appreciate the implications of the links between:

- the 1989 Children Act, which encompasses child protection procedures, extends responsibilities for special needs to other statutory agencies, such as social services, and thus calls for increased collaboration between practitioners;
- the 'Rumbold Report' (Rumbold, 1990), which examines preschool experience and inevitably considers requisites for school learning;
- the Elton Report (Elton, 1989) on discipline in schools, which contained pervasive recommendations applicable to all schools, (explored in Chapter 4);
- the International Convention on the Rights of the Child adopted by the United Nations General Assembly in 1989, and subsequently ratified by an increasing number of countries; its significance for educationalists is that a number of the articles of the Convention declare a commitment to educational opportunities as well as upholding a number of rights pertaining to children with disabilities

Another initiative, of which this book forms part, is the growing number of titles in the Cassell series 'Special Needs in Ordinary Schools', which collectively provide a set of statements or blueprints for practice and which attest to an accumulation of expertise written by and available to practitioners.

This second edition is emphatically not a 'new' book; it sets out to incorporate recent legislation and initiatives into the earlier framework. Naturally, for reasons of space and succinctness, a number of references have vanished, replaced by others of greater pith and moment. The fundamental commitment to equal opportunities and collective responsibility remains.

Chapter 1 sets out to locate the concept of special educational needs and, whilst acknowledging the elusive and at times illusory nature of the concept, attempts an unequivocal statement about the learning and emotional needs of every child. The ideological difficulties in deriving formulae about 'special educational needs' are examined in reference to broader perspectives on primary education and with a view to some sort of synthesis.

Throughout the book the expressed commitment is towards the evolution and adoption of 'collective responsibility' for children with identified special educational needs. This encompasses, without question, the involvement and contribution of their parents and caregivers within community contexts. These dimensions are particularly addressed in Chapter 2.

Chapters 3 and 4 single out two major areas of concern to many teachers and others in education, namely learning and behaviour difficulties. A balance is sought between formulating, in practical terms, strategies that can be adopted to tackle identified problems whilst, at the same time, reiterating how context-specific, even relative, these issues can be. The broader, 'school as a system' context is examined in Chapter 5, which also sets out the 'collective responsibility' idea in workable terms. No blueprint for educational action nowadays would be complete without discussion on staff development and support and the inservice training needs of teachers, and this is the focus of Chapter 6. Since the preceding chapters provide the basis for a school policy for special educational needs, Chapter 7 sets out to formulate and discuss the elements which could form such a policy.

Chapter 8 aims, however briefly, to provide a bridge between primary and secondary settings and discusses ways of bringing about a smooth transition for those children who may be especially vulnerable at this potentially critical time.

It is hoped that the readership of this book, and indeed of this series, will be wide. A fair amount of professional sophistication is assumed and, for readers who want back-up and confirmation of contemporary thinking and practice, a considerable number of references are provided. Chapters 3 and 4 carry the most references, for these are areas with direct implications for follow-up work. Texts relevant for further reading or practical application are asterisked.

In keeping with my own views, there is no intentionally sexist language. All allusions to children and adults are he/she, his/her, etc.

Finally, a word about children, who are, indeed, the 'subject matter' of this book. Running throughout this book is the assumption that we address ourselves to all children, irrespective of background and circumstance, yet we live in an era when, justifiably, we perceive that our professional responsibilities towards children from ethnic minority backgrounds must include action that is affirmative. We must be sensitive towards the 'distinctive needs' (Wolfendale, 1983) of a number of children whose learnings needs are compounded in this era by their overwhelming need to benefit from, and be part of, an educational system that has operated for many, many years without particular regard to individuals or their cultural backgrounds.

My declared commitment is, then, to the provision of equal opportunities, and to the eradication of any unintentional educational practice that further disadvantages children who are already coming to terms with the functional use of more than one language, who are reconciling, coping with, and responding to at times, disparate cultural and religious frameworks (Boyd, 1989). These do not have to be 'problems' (a word that confirms the onus on the child and his/her family) but they do have to be 'issues' to be dealt with as part of collective responsibility, which is a cornerstone philosophy of this book.

I go along with the basic premise contained in the Swann Report (1985), which unequivocally states that reponsibility for providing equal access and opportunities, without prejudice, belongs to each and every school and educational institution within each and every local education authority. The Swann Report's conception of 'education for all' embraces what it terms 'the realities of British society now and in the future, that a variety of ethnic groups with their own distinct lifestyles and value systems will be living together' (Swann Report, p. 324). This, then, provides the broadest backcloth of all to this book.

REFERENCES

Boyd, J. (1989) *Equality Issues in Primary Schools*. London: Paul Chapman.
Elton, R. (Chair) (1989) *Discipline in Schools*. London: HMSO.
Rumbold, A. (Chair) (1990) *Starting with Quality*. Report of the Committee of Inquiry into the quality of educational experience offered to 3- and 4-year-olds. London: HMSO.
Swann, M. (Chair) (1985) *Education for All*. Report of the Committee of Inquiry into the Education of Children from Ethnic Minority Groups. London: HMSO.
Wolfendale, S. (1983) *Parental Participation in Children's Development and Education*. London: Gordon & Breach.

—1————————————

Reformulating special needs and realigning primary practice

This book is about attitude and action. It is for teachers and about teachers, and it has been written on behalf of children in primary schools.

Based on the notion that all children are special, it is a book that sets out to reconcile two major traditions in British education. One is the tradition of primary schooling, with its ideologies and well-attested pedagogies. The other tradition is that of special education, which, over the period of this century, has evolved its own separate identity and educational philosophy. Between these dominant traditions has been a third strand: the grey, nebulous area of remedial education, uneasily straddling these distinctive worlds of mainstream primary and special education. It has been allied more closely to mainstream whilst simultaneously deriving some of its identity from certain of the precepts and practices of special education.

The separate traditions permeate education – they are to be found in the literature, in library classifications, in inservice provision, in job titles, in educational research. A reconciliation is timely. The Warnock Committee pronounced that a meaningful distinction between remedial and special education could no longer be maintained, and this, of course, was a statement en route towards a reaffirmation of the principle of integrated and fully comprehensive education. Likewise, 11 years earlier the Plowden Committee, within its remit to consider the 'whole subject of primary education', was concerned with all children in primary schools and how their learning needs could be met.

An alignment between 'best' practice in primary and in special education is called for. As schools embrace the equality of opportunity inherent in the anti-discriminatory educational policies espoused by an increasing number of local education authorities, so the hard-won expertise in devising effective curricula in primary schools needs to be matched by and married to the equally hard-won expertise in remedial and special education.

Educational aims as propounded in textbooks, by LEAs and by schools have represented a knitting together of the differing strands of

1

education within an 'education for all' philosophy. The HMI discussion document *The Curriculum from 5-16* (DES, 1985), in acknowledging the commonality of educational aims, stated:

> Whatever means a school uses to translate its aims into everyday curricular terms, and whatever means it uses to provide appropriately for pupils of different ages and abilities, broad aims . . . should underlie its day-to-day work in respect of all its pupils. (p. 3)

This turned out to be a precursor to the stated aims of the National Curriculum (NCC, 1989a, 1989b, 1990).

But beyond the rhetoric lies the task of translating aims into sound pedagogic practice that provides for the universality of all children's needs as well as for the specificity of each child's needs, and for the overwhelming majority whose paramount educational need is to be educated in local schools. This chapter is intended to provide the conceptual underpinning of an integrated approach to meeting special educational needs in primary schools, and to set the scene for subsequent chapters that explore the application of these views in practice.

EFFECTS OF THE DEBATE ON SPECIAL NEEDS

The opening sentence of this chapter referred to attitude. As schools interact with, and are a part of, their communities, it is the aspiration of those in favour of integrated education that greater tolerance and understanding of disability, 'deviance', and differing backgrounds will eventually inform and influence a wider public.

Case studies abound (Thomas, 1982; Topliss, 1982) as to the entrenched and fearful prejudices of people towards 'difference' of any kind, yet 'difference' itself is shown, in surveys, to be discretely defined and usually relative. For example, a survey in Yorkshire into attitudes to Down's syndrome revealed misunderstanding, even hostility, to mental handicap (Sinson, 1985). Polls on attitudes by a (largely) able-bodied public into disability (mental and physical) reported by McConkey and McCormack (1983) confirm equivocal and ambiguous attitudes; misunderstanding and sympathy co-exist uneasily. McConkey and McCormack are confident that public attitudes to, and acceptance of, disability can be altered, and their book brims with practical group and community activities designed to bring about change. Rieser and Mason (1990) trace the history of pejorative, rejecting, stereotyping attitudes and practice towards disabled children and adults in a book that celebrates diversity and firmly places disability within the context of equal opportunities. They maintain that the issues are relevant to everyone in schools as well as in society.

One unit in their book outlines practical work that can be done in class as an integral part of the National Curriculum, to foster reflectiveness, change attitudes and foster sensitive, responsive behaviour towards children with disability.

The educational community, in part by virtue of legislative change, is charged with a particular responsibility to open the debate locally and keep it vibrant. Some local education authorities have taken this responsibility seriously and have produced consultative documents on special needs, policies and provision. The opening up of debate, the abolition of statutory categories of handicap, and the changed terminology do seem to be bringing about attitude change (e.g. the chronicled readiness of an increasing number of nursery, infant, and first schools to admit Down's syndrome children). But the change in nomenclature has created a dilemma that concerns the very term 'special educational needs' (Galloway, 1985) in the necessarily arbitrary nature of the cut-off point of 'special' (Gipps, Goldstein and Gross, 1985) and the inescapable, and not always benign, influence of social interests and vested power upon the consideration of 'special' needs (Ford, Mongon and Whelan, 1982; Barton and Tomlinson, 1984).

These crucial and semantic issues have not been resolved by the advent of the Education Reform Act, despite pronouncements concerning the entitlement of *all* children to the National Curriculum, including children with special educational needs, for whom the Curriculum should not be suspended or modified (DES, 1989a). Rather, Local Management of Schools (LMS) formula-funding arrangements, which ensure the diversion of certain funds to children with identified special needs and earmarking of LEA moneys to children who have been assessed under the 1981 Education Act Section 5 procedures, encourage the perpetuation of disability labels. During 1991 professionals working in this area noted, informally (official statistics had not at the time of writing been nationally collated), an increase in the number of children with statements. This confirms fears that with the LMS arrangements a 'Section 5' assessment would be perceived as the route to guarantee special funding for 'special' children. Thus the divisions, if not the categories, are perpetuated and the special educational continuum advocated in the Warnock Report is no nearer achievement.

Likewise the principle, not to mention the practice, of integration is put at risk for the same reasons, and also because despite the requirement that schools wishing to become grant-maintained must state in their DES submission what their arrangements for special educational needs are going to be, these schools will be allowed a degree of latitude and autonomy. The useful advice contained in such publications as

NARE's (Ford, 1989) is likely to be wasted in educational settings where there is neither the will nor the means to effect integration.

The implacable paradox remains: there are some children who, at any one time, will be deemed to 'have' special educational needs, a minority of whom will be accorded the 'protection of a statement' (via 1981 Education Act Section 5 assessment procedures) – but , conversely, *all* children are special (Brennan, 1982). The humanitarian intention in singling out children who are said to be in need of special, different, extra provision is at odds with the perfidious effects of the label. Ensuring special attention for designated children means that those children are seen as representative of a type (special versus non-special needs). From that acknowledgement it is but a short step to categorising once more.

These contradictions bedevil all of us working in education and on behalf of children. On the one hand, it is vital to safeguard educational interests to ensure maximum protection of children with 'disabilities'. On the other hand, we are constrained by our basic human tendency to group and classify all manner of phenomena, including children in our charge. In common currency still are categories such as: disadvantaged; working-class; coming from an ethnic minority; maladjusted; slow learner; and so on. The point has been forcibly made by writers cited above and others that the maintenance of such descriptions ensures the perpetuation of the within-child deficit model (which ascribes the problem to the child and not to external factors). Further, such grouping ensures that an individual child is less a unique *subject*, worthy of individual consideration, than an *object*, representative of a type or class and showing relevant characteristics. Schools are then absolved from critically reappraising conditions for learning, and the education service from rationalising provision.

Indeed, the legal process of assessing, discovering, identifying, and pronouncing a special need acute enough to warrant the 'protection of a statement' has generated a whole industry within education. Procedural manuals proliferate, and within each LEA there is a proper, rule-bound specification for the implementation of these processes: see Solity and Raybould (1988) for their guidance to teachers.

In order for the actions with which this book is concerned to be robust and credible, these reminders of the pitfalls of groupings and labelling have had to be given. Before the discussion in this chapter moves on, the point has forcibly to be made that the term 'special educational needs' must not be used to differentiate individual children from one another nor groups from one another. It has to be used, as it was intended, to ensure a match between the learning needs at any one time of an individual child and the best provision and resources that can be made available for that child. But the dilemma in differentiating between 'special' (temporary, particular, distinctive) and universal learning needs (in the sense of rights of access to all available learning opportunities) of all children persists. Norwich (1990), in subjecting this match between needs and provision to piercing and detailed scrutiny, highlights an anomaly:

> identifying a need implies that some condition is necessary for achieving a standard. In other words, what is needed is provision to meet that need . . . advice about special educational needs will necessarily involve advice about provision required. This makes it difficult to understand why professionals are supposed to distinguish between the child's special needs and the provision required. (p. 131)

Indeed, this matter continues to exercise such practitioners as educational psychologists.

TOWARDS A FRAMEWORK OF SUPPORT IN PRIMARY SCHOOLS

This section of the chapter contains the nub of the case for aligning primary and special education. It will pay attention to teacher education, the concept of learning needs, and the development of support networks within schools, and will examine the rationale of intervention. It will aim to present a view of primary education that is indivisible from, and indeed provides, the context for special provision.

One of the factors governing the temptation to group and label is an ignorance of the 'condition' that seems, at any one time, to obtain for a child, e.g. a learning difficulty, a behaviour problem, and the consequent uncertainty as to how to cope.

The Warnock Report recognised that as class teachers are so central to children's school lives, training and support should enable them to recognise individual children's learning needs and respond appropriately. An integrated and truly comprehensive system demands more of teachers, however. Here, again, is a potential dilemma. Teachers can expect children who hitherto have been in special schools to be in mainstream primaries, within any one of several variations of integration (Hodgson, Clunies-Ross and Hegarty, 1984). So they are expected to have some familiarity with ranges of learning difficulty (from moderate to severe); with degrees of physical and sensory handicap – and to respond sensitively. At the same time they cannot be experts on a whole variety of serious and complex disabilities that may require special aetiological knowledge as well as specific equipment and teaching methods. Likewise, teachers within the special education community have long been protective of children in their charge, and have themselves evolved specialisms in the realms of educating and caring for mildly and profoundly handicapped children. Can they, along with teachers in primary schools, be reassured that their charges' best interests are served in integrated settings?

Reform in education is not an overnight phenomenon. Where reforming measures combine legislative frameworks, shifts in resource allocation, changes in attitudes and expectation, there needs to be a phased programme towards goals specified for, and achievable at, each stage.

Teacher education is, therefore, a particular priority at the early stages of a programme. There needs to be a rapprochement between the relative teaching experience and educational knowledge of teachers from primary and from special education settings, so that each can inform and support the other. It is consistent with the intent of integration that knowledge about special needs, from mild, to moderate, to acute and medically dependent conditions, should be made accessible to mainstream teachers. On the basis of being better informed and knowledgeable about where specialist support is available, they are then in a more secure and personally comfortable position to meet children's learning needs.

Jones (1985), in discussing attitudes to disability and the requisites within teacher training for bringing about change, cautions against cosmetic approaches that duck the most fundamental requisite of all – namely, that the responsibility for ensuring that children's needs are met in schools is conjoint, collective and no longer the exclusive property of specially assigned teachers and other experts.

This theme will be elaborated and illustrated in this chapter and throughout this book.

THE NOTION OF COLLECTIVE RESPONSIBILITY

Even before, and certainly since, the era that saw the publication of the Plowden Report (1967), we have been accustomed to remedial teaching expertise growing up alongside generalist subject teaching at primary level. Children in need of remedial help have been siphoned off to units or small groups, injected with their dose of remedial reading and returned to their classes.

The relative ineffectiveness of such discrete jabs of remediation and the lack of generalisability of performance was commented on in the Bullock Report (1975), which laid down one of the rubrics of successful intervention with children's reading difficulties – namely, an across-the-curriculum approach to language. This was one of the first calls for co-ordinated provision within schools and paved the way for a greater assumption of responsibility by other teachers who had contact with 'failing' children.

Even with a broader conception of special needs, and the gradual abandonment of the term 'remedial' in educational circles, there would be the danger that designated 'special needs teachers' (often called co-ordinators) would be regarded as the repository of responsibility as well as expertise. This book, and this series, takes a pluralist view of special needs, wherein the perception of a child's unique special need is that it merges into and is not easily separable from his or her universal needs. Not only does a separatist line militate against a 'pure' principle of integration, but, more pragmatically, the complex web of a child's needs are such that no one teacher can adequately meet them.

We have to acknowledge that to posit special needs is to have to provide for their being met in ordinary classrooms. It also follows that only a network of personnel and provision can ensure this. So we must abandon the old unitary view of teaching in primary schools, where the onus of responsibility is put personally onto individual class teachers. We have to move towards establishing within schools task-forces of teachers and others who have explicit and differential responsibility for carrying out a school's policy on special needs.

So, for class teachers, from their initial training onwards, special needs would not be viewed as something grafted onto the curriculum, tacked on for a minority of children. They would be able readily to accept that establishing classroom conditions conducive to learning by all children is central to their task. Likewise, the class teacher would be supported by other teachers, in terms of curriculum planning, co-teaching, monitoring, review, and in and out of school liaison. The structures within the school would also facilitate the carrying out of special needs policies and would enable collective responsibility to be exercised. The strengthening of powers and responsibilities of governing bodies via the Education Acts of 1981, 1986 and 1988 reinforces the collective principle.

A corporate endeavour, too, would act in the interests of efficiency and cost effectiveness, facts of life that have to be considered. It would encourage the best use of the panoply of outside-school services which exist to back up and supplement school-based provision, but which are not always readily accessible to class teachers and, moreover, threaten to reduce the overall responsibility that should be the schools'.

Within a broader context still, the responsibility towards effective implementation of a special needs policy has to be shared with the LEA advisory and administrative staff. The theme of a 'network of services' is explored in Chapter 5.

A CHILD-CENTRED VIEW OF MEETING SPECIAL NEEDS IN THE PRIMARY SCHOOL

In her critique of developmental psychology and child-centred pedagogy, Walkerdine (1984) tackles attitudes and practices that she says characterise the British primary school, which is

> taken to be a paradigm of practice for a considerable proportion of the Western World. Here, children are to be enabled to develop at their own pace, to work individually, to be free and to grow up into rational adults. (p. 153)

But to question the concept, as Walkerdine does, for failing, in its translation into practice, to liberate children and unshackle them from constraints in the social domain, is to presuppose that structure, organised teaching and learning were never explicitly part of the child-centred ideology. That ideology itself has been prey to fashion; such that the learning by discovery approach was seen as all or none, despite discussions by Stones (1970) and others as to its many-faceted nature. As the Plowden Report put it, rather starkly, ' "finding out" has proved to be better for children than "being told" ' (Plowden, 1967, para. 1233, p. 460).

This polarisation is also criticised by Alexander (1984), who writes:

> My argument is that the primary school's strengths in respect of climate and interpersonal relations are sometimes offset by weaknesses in respect of curriculum and pedagogy. . . . As ideology, child-centredness may be effective; as educational rationale it is sometimes deficient. (p. 15)

The essence of a child-centred approach seems to have been the emphasis upon encouraging whole-child development within a 'progressive' frame (Galton, Simon and Croll, 1980), where a child was less coerced into learning than encouraged towards the learning opportunities made available. In short, it made the child the *subject* rather than the *object*, to be slotted into a pre-determined curriculum.

Suspicions about the effectiveness of such an approach, *laissez-faire* at worst, random at best and less amenable to measurement, have been fuelled by the increasing adoption, certainly in remedial and special settings, of objectives-based curricula. These are founded on the idea that it is in children's best learning interests, particularly for 'slow' learners, to be in receipt of a curriculum (for reading, spelling, handwriting, number and language) (Cameron, 1981) that has been task-analysed. Longer-term goals and short-term targets can then be devised for a child whose entry skills are first appraised on a criterion-referenced placement (attainment) test (see Chapter 3).

What is proposed at this point is a redefinition of child-centred education to take account of each child's learning needs, and acknowledge the 'special' nature of these, in so far as it becomes the collective responsibility of all in the school to ensure that these are met. That is, instead of children being perceived to 'fail' the curriculum (be behind in maths by the end of the year, have a reading age lower than chronological age, for example), a given child is enabled to reach realistic and achievable learning goals devised for (and with) that child from a rich and diverse bank of educational experiences.

So the notion of a 'remedial' approach for a particular child, where the provision (a DATAPAC programme, a peer-tutored, paired reading programme, for example) is uneasily appended to the child's other curriculum experiences, becomes superseded by a different conception.

That provision (examples given just above) that has been worked out by the team (see Chapter 5) as being appropriate to meet the child's learning needs integrally, becomes part of the broader curriculum opportunity for the child, so that she or he can take maximum advantage of what is on offer within the school. How often has a 'remedial' child, a 'slow learner', been deprived of and cut off from the rest of the peer group by virtue of reading and learning difficulties? The only match that has been made with his or her needs has been to provide a discrete remedial programme for a finite number of minutes per day, or times per week, based on the concept of 'failure'.

The creation of the National Curriculum in theory facilitates the realisation of this child-centred model. With its central stem and attendant features of attainment targets, levels, profile components and programmes of study it is a conceptually neat idea. Children's achievement and progress are made visible and measurable by means of the National Curriculum structures and teacher-based points of assessment. What reduces the potential of the National Curriculum as a vehicle that would best promote equality of opportunity of children with special needs (learning difficulties in particular), is that the ultimately norm-referenced nature of the Standard Assessment Tasks (SATs) means that the reality of failure cannot be averted. Although this likelihood will tend to dominate as each Key Stage SAT draws near, in the day-to-day and week-by-week of school life it is in fact increasingly likely that children's individual learning needs will be catered for. Indeed, as we shall see in Chapter 3 in particular, approaches and programmes have been devised within the framework of the National Curriculum. A starting point that remains totally consistent with the child-centred view propagated here is an appraisal of the child's 'strengths and weaknesses', as the balance-sheet of individual competencies in childhood is usually described.

The need to assess a child's 'strengths and weaknesses' has been stressed in recent years, in order to

1. escape from the deficit model
2. use the strengths (learning assets) to compensate for the weaknesses (learning difficulties)
3. maintain motivation by acknowledging these strengths whilst working on the weaknesses.

However, the idea that a composite assessment of a child's strengths and weaknesses can be translated into teaching goals across the primary curriculum has not yet caught on widely in practice. As long as we maintain distinct areas of responsibility (remedial/advisory teacher and educational psychologist concerned with failure and remediation; class teacher concerned with the rest of the curriculum) we are unlikely to be able to cater adequately for the totality of a child's educational needs.

A child's learning strengths can be defined as: comprising those areas of the curriculum that the child enjoys, is motivated to attend to, participate and progress in, and to which he or she brings an appropriate learning style. These assets need to be capitalised upon, across and within each subject and curriculum area, and a learning programme must be devised that embraces these areas.

However, the whole debate about the appropriateness of the delivery and content of the primary curriculum resurfaced during 1991 and 1992 (see Alexander, 1991; Alexander, Rose and Woodhead, 1992) and is under scrutiny from the National Curriculum Council, which is examining the available evidence in the areas of teaching/learning styles, classroom organisation and management. Outcomes and recommendations emanating from these reviews have an inevitable bearing upon 'special needs' teaching.

What is proposed here as being consistent with a child-centred view of meeting special needs in primary settings is the idea of a *learning profile*. This would be devised for each child, based on an assessment of 'entry' skills evident at the time of assessment, matched with appropriate short and longer-term learning goals, and regularly reviewed by key staff and parents. This formulation is explored further in Chapter 3.

One final word in this introduction to a redefinition of a child-centred view to meeting special needs, and one which is by way of a trailer to Chapter 3. This refers to the place of norm-referenced assessment. Reference to the norm (via tests, checklists, and rating scales) is only applicable if it illuminates how to help a child. If it is not criterion-referenced, a test serves no function. An IQ test is a sterile measure that cannot provide indicators of the next teaching and learning goals. Even a reading age (Vincent and de la Mare, 1985) is notional. An assessment must work *for* and not *against* a child, i.e. an external yardstick should not be used as a measure of the 'success' or 'failure' of the child, and so, as earlier indicated, we must remain vigilant that the SATs work for and not against children's interests.

THE WIDER CONTEXT TO CHILDREN'S NEEDS: ENSURING RIGHTS

Whilst the preface to this book staked out the territory to be covered, this first chapter aspires to impart a statement of intent in respect of the concept of needs and a reformulation of this within a mainstream primary context. In the discussion on 'needs' the idea has lain embedded that it is the right of each child to have his or her learning and other needs fully met in school.

This fundamental right is now enshrined in National Curriculum documents (NCC, 1989b, c), which spell out the *entitlement* of all children to 'share in the curriculum', though NCC (1989b) emphasises that this right 'does not automatically ensure access to it, nor progress within it' (p. 1). This cautionary note goes on:

> Achieving maximum access and subsequent progress for pupils with S.E.N. will challenge the co-operation, understanding and planning skills of teachers, support agencies, parents, governors and many others. (pp. 1–2)

The ideology of this book embraces, however, the consideration not only of children's rights but of those of teachers, parents, and other participants in educational processes. This sounds as if the remit is so broad that the focus of the message will be diffused. It will, though, be a central tenet that children's needs and their rights can be appraised by reference to adults of significance in their lives in so far as their influence impinges upon schooling.

Roaf and Bines (1989), too, place children's rights and equality issues within broader contexts of significant adults' rights, including adults with disabilities whose unique perspectives confer legitimacy upon their views about control of services and anti-discrimination legislation. Democratisation of the education service has, on the one hand, been enhanced by the 'parent power' mechanisms and governors' duties inherent in recent educational legislation; on the other hand, diffusion of provision brought about by opportunities for schools to 'opt out' and increased centralisation threatened by the weakened role of LEAs may militate against decision-making being a coalition of local vested interests. Even if a consensus is not achievable in all circumstances, at least local representatives have an understanding of the relativities of local need and commensurate provision.

The idea of collective responsibility has already been aired, and this is in keeping with the ecological perspectives to be discussed in Chapter 2. Implicit in the effective functioning of the actors in the primary scenarios that are portrayed throughout the book are some fundamental features:

- that the actors' (for example, teachers, parents, support personnel, governors) roles, functions, and responsibilities have been properly defined, clarified, and delineated so that they are comfortable in them.
- that the relationships between and amongst these principal actors have equally been delineated and made explicit, so that when it comes to the exercising of roles and responsibilities to do with special needs provision, these demarcations facilitate the application of policy.

These remarks are not intended to be exhortatory. They are prompted by the wisdom of retrospect: looking back over time as an involved educationalist within remedial and special education, one cannot but be struck by the proliferation of personnel and provision that emerged in response to immediate need, rather than being planned as a longer-term, more measured and considered response to anticipated problems or articulated educational philosophies.

We have enough accumulated knowledge and expertise, within both primary and remedial/special settings, to be able, now, to plan provision and training that incorporate adequate consideration of job satisfaction for all parties. So, in this book, attention will be paid to the professional needs of teachers and others who contribute to the life of schools. This includes consideration, too, of the self-determination of children in being involved in setting their own learning goals, and self-appraisal and self-management by teachers. Braun and Lasher (1978) refer to the role definition that is needed when 'mainstreaming' children with special needs, and Campbell (1985), within the context of British primary education, makes a case for the evolution of the 'collegial' primary school. Barton and Smith (1989) exhort primary schools to broaden the basis of their traditional child-centred approaches to encompass rights and equality principles within a collaborative spirit.

TRACING THE RECENT PROGRESS OF SPECIAL NEEDS IN MAINSTREAM SCHOOLS

Reformulating concepts of special needs necessitates a brief examination as to how special educational needs in mainstream schools have fared since the implementation of the 1981 Education Act from April 1983. Superficially we find a situation akin to the proverbial curate's egg: 'good in parts'. Goacher *et al.* (1988) confirm a scene of transition and adaptation during the 1980s, with a tremendous amount of commitment and innovatory practice (in areas to do with curriculum, awareness-raising, INSET, support staff) combined with inertia, sluggish bureaucratic procedures and inadequate resourcing.

The Select Committee Report on the 1981 Education Act (1987) confirmed that meeting special educational needs has become a more integral part of the work of primary and secondary schools (para. 13). Echoing the debate about definition of special needs, it stated, 'there is a strong case for more guidance about identifying the wide range of special educational needs and about when a statement of such needs might be required' (para. 26). Presciently (since the National Curriculum had not yet been proposed), the Report also pointed out that 'there is a difficult borderline between what schools provide for all pupils and the special arrangements which they may make for some pupils with the wider range of special educational needs' (para. 30).

An HMI survey into pupils with special educational needs in ordinary schools undertaken between 1988 and 1989 (DES, 1989b) likewise confirmed the higher profile for special needs in schools. Those carrying out the survey reported that half the schools visited (55 primary, 42 secondary in 38 LEAs) had reviewed their identification and monitoring procedures, organisation, classroom practice, staff training, and had developed a whole-school policy. They advised, however, in conclusion, that one-third of the schools visited needed to review their special needs provision in order to give pupils 'full and proper' access to the National Curriculum.

A companion HMI survey (DES, 1990c) looked at provision for primary-aged pupils with statements of special educational needs in mainstream schools and was critical on a number of counts: e.g. curriculum differentiation, poor review procedures and the need for better material provision, including environmental adaptations to accommodate pupils with physical or sensory handicaps.

Finally, HMI produced a document (DES, 1990a) summarising current special needs issues and looking prospectively towards the 1990s. This, whilst endorsing the principle and the evident shift towards integration (but not a sufficient degree of shift according to a 1991 survey carried out by CSIE), noted: 'whilst there is scope for further integration of pupils with special needs in ordinary schools, this needs to be undertaken with great care, particularly with respect to curriculum breadth and balance' (p. 31).

RATIONALE FOR INTERVENTION: SQUARING UP TO THE NATIONAL CURRICULUM TO ENSURE A CENTRAL PLACE FOR SPECIAL NEEDS

Intervention in children's learning is usually perceived to be the provision of something over, above, and additional to the curriculum, and epitomised by programmes, kits and 'packages' that have come to be associated with remedial approaches to the 'slow learner', the 'retarded', the 'underachiever'. The definition of 'intervention' by Anderson (quoted in Wolfendale and Bryans, 1979) is compatible with the idea of providing something additional to, or parallel with, the main curriculum, but could also be seen to apply to education itself. The definition given by Anderson is that intervention is 'a conscious and purposeful set of actions intended to change or influence the anticipated course of development' (Wolfendale and Bryans, 1979, p. 18).

On the premise that much learning is incidental, and that the match between teaching input and learning output (children's performance) is imperfectly understood, intervention is perceived as an intentional teaching and learning programme comprising goals, the achievement of which can be measured. This view of curriculum planning is consistent with the child-centred view of meeting children's needs described above. In this conception the distinction between remedial and nonremedial is blurred if not abolished, as intervention becomes education for all children.

The pluralist position outlined by Norwich (1990) accords with the unfolding themes of this book and with a view of intervention that encompasses National Curriculum directives, with scope for modifying or building upon it in such a way as to promote effective learning, wherein the child is challenged positively.

Realistically, as long as modification (DES, 1989a) is not seen as a 'cop out' and a slippery slope to an alternative, remedial-style curriculum, it offers scope for flexibly using the National Curriculum itself to offer the requisite broad and balanced curriculum. This conception retains a continuing close relationship of the learner to the core and foundation subjects as well as the broader curriculum and also builds in to this notion of intervention other key features such as agreeing teaching style, and appraising the learning and social environments (see Chapter 3).

Despite the positive commitment to these ideals, it has to be acknowledged that there are intrinsic contradictions in this whole area. The concern is expressed by the writers in Daniels and Ware (1990) that NCC and SEAC documents imply that learning by pupils with special educational needs (especially those with learning difficulties) is qualitatively different from others and that learning proceeds along a linear route and can therefore be measured simply at fixed points along the continuum.

The National Union of Teachers points out that the web of cross-referenced attainment targets and levels of achievement represents the complexity of real learning onto which social, motivational, ecological forces impinge. Daniels (1990) perceives that there are conflicting influences from different vested interests and mixed messages teachers are receiving about the status to be accorded to special needs children, relative to the other considerable demands on their time.

This chapter has attempted to align the historic child-centred aims of primary education with a changing conception of special educational needs that eschews separatist, remedial traditions and embraces whole-child perspectives as part of a commitment to equality of opportunity. The central place advocated for special needs is explored in subsequent chapters.

REFERENCES

Alexander, R. (1984) *Primary Teaching*. London: Holt, Rinehart & Winston.

Alexander, R. (1991) *Primary Education in Leeds: A Report*. School of Education, University of Leeds, Leeds LS2 9JT.

Alexander, R., Rose, J. and Woodhead, C. (1992) *Curriculum Organisation and Classroom Practice in Primary Schools: A Discussion Paper*. London: DES.

Barton, L. and Smith, M. (1989) 'Equality, rights and primary education'. In Roaf and Bines, op. cit., ch. 6.

Barton, L. and Tomlinson, S. (eds) (1984) *Special Education and Social Interests*. Beckenham: Croom Helm.

Braun, S. and Lasher, M. (1978) *Are You Ready to Mainstream?* London: Charles E. Merrill.

Brennan, W. (1982) *Changing Special Education*. Milton Keynes: Open University Press.

Bullock, A. (Chair) (1975) *A Language for Life*. London: HMSO.

Cameron, R.J. (ed.) (1981) Curriculum development. Curriculum objectives issue, *Journal of Remedial Education* 16 (4) (November).

Campbell, R.J. (1985) *Developing the Primary School Curriculum*. Eastbourne: Holt, Rinehart & Winston.

CSIE (Centre for Studies on Integration in Education), 415 Edgware Road, London NW2 6NB. Tel. (081) 452 8642.

Daniels, H. (1990) 'Implications for special educational needs in the ordinary school'. In Daniels and Ware, op. cit., ch. 4.

Daniels, H. and Ware, J. (eds) (1990) *Special Educational Needs and the National Curriculum*. London: Kogan Page/University of London Institute of Education.

DES (1985) *The Curriculum from 5–16*. London: HMSO.

DES (1989a) *Assessments and Statements of Special Educational Needs: Procedures within the Education, Health and Social Services*, Circular 22/89. London: DES.

DES (1989b) *A Survey of Pupils with Special Educational Needs in Ordinary Schools, 1988–89*. London: HMSO.

DES (1989c) *National Curriculum: From Polity to Practice*. London: HMSO.

DES (1990a). *Provision for Primary-aged Pupils with Statements of Special Educational Needs in Mainstream Schools, January–July 1989*. London: HMSO.

DES (1990b) *Special Needs Issues: A Survey by HMI*, London: HMSO.

Dessent, A. (1983) 'Who is responsible for children with special needs?' In Booth, T. and Potts, P. (eds) *Integrating Special Education*. Oxford: Basil Blackwell, ch. 6.

Ford, B. (1989) *Making Integration Work*. Stafford: National Association for Remedial Education (NARE).

Ford, J., Mongon, D. and Whelan, M. (1982) *Special Education and Social Control*. London: Routledge & Kegan Paul.

Galloway, D. (1985) *Schools, Pupils and Special Educational Needs*. Beckenham: Croom Helm.

Galton, M., Simon, B. and Croll, P. (1980) *Inside the Primary Classroom*. London: Routledge & Kegan Paul.

Gipps, C., Goldstein, H. and Gross, H. (1985) Twenty per cent with special needs: another legacy from Cyril Burt. *Journal of Remedial Education* 20 (2).

Goacher, B., Evans, J., Welton, J. and Wedell, K. (1988) *Policy and Provision for Special Educational Needs*. London: Cassell.

Hodgson, A., Clunies-Ross, L. and Hegarty, S. (1984) *Learning Together: Teaching Pupils with Special Educational Needs in the Ordinary School*. Windsor: NFER-Nelson.

Jones, N. (1985) 'Attitudes to disability: a training objective'. In Sayer, J. and Jones, N. (eds) *Teacher Training and Special Educational Needs*, ch. 2. Beckenham: Croom Helm.

McConkey, R. and McCormack, B. (1983) *Breaking Barriers, Educating People about Disability*. Human Horizons Series. London: Souvenir Press.

McCreesh, J. and Maher, A. (1974) *Remedial Education: Objectives and Techniques*. London: Ward Lock Educational.

NCC (1989a) *Guidance No. 1: A Framework for the Primary Curriculum*. All York: National Curriculum Council.

NCC (1989b) *Guidance No. 2: A Curriculum for All: Special Educational Needs in the National Curriculum*.

NCC (1989c) Newsletter No. 5 (on SEN).

NCC (1990) *Guidance No. 3: The Whole Curriculum*.

Norwich, B. (1990) *Reappraising Special Needs Education*. London: Cassell.

Plowden, B. (Chair) (1967) *Children and Their Primary Schools*. London: HMSO.

Rieser, R. and Mason, M. (1990) *Disability, Equality in the Classroom: A Human Rights Issue*. London: ILEA.

Roaf, C. and Bines, H. (eds) (1989) *Needs, Rights and Opportunities*. Lewes: Falmer Press.

Select Committee (1987) *Report on the 1981 Education Act*, vol. 1. London: HMSO.

Sinson, J. (1985) *Attitudes to Down's Syndrome: An Investigation of Attitudes to Mental Handicap in Urban and Rural Yorkshire*. Mental Health Foundation, 8 Hallam Street, London W1N 6DH.

Solity, J. and Raybould, E. (1989) *A Teacher's Guide to Special Needs: A Positive Response to the 1981 Education Act*. Milton Keynes: Open University Press.

Stones, E. (1970) *Readings in Educational Psychology*. London: Methuen.

Thomas, D. (1982) *The Experience of Handicap*. London: Methuen.

Topliss, E. (1982) *Social Responses to Handicap*. London: Longman.

Vincent, D. and de la Mare, M. (1985) *New Macmillan Reading Analysis*. Basingstoke: Macmillan.

Walkerdine, V. (1984) 'Developmental psychology, the child-centred pedagogy: the insertion of Piaget into early education'. In Henriques, J., Hollway, W., Urwin, C., Venn, C. and Walkerdine, V. (eds) *Changing the Subject*. London: Methuen.

Wolfendale, S. and Bryans, T. (1979) *Identification of Learning Difficulties: A Model for Intervention*. Stafford: National Association for Remedial Education.

Home and school milieux for meeting children's needs

It is an opportune time to look back and chart developments in home–school links since the publication of the Plowden Report and its seemingly simple assertion that 'by involving the parents, the children may be helped' (Plowden, 1967, para. 114). In fact, that assertion was based on the early findings from the American programme Head Start, as well as a heart-felt conviction by the Plowden committee that, as parents are children's 'primary educators', then professionals' support of their direct involvement with their children's development and education could only be beneficial.

What constitutes 'benefit' to children in these terms was closely examined in a review of developments in parental involvement (Wolfendale, 1983). In that book, I set out a rationale to this growing area and put forward recommendations for the development of LEA and school policies on working with parents.

This chapter sets out to draw together a number of recent and current initiatives within primary and special education that bear testimony to the effectiveness of such co-operation. They also provide us with clues as to how successfully to instigate and maintain a way of working which had traditionally been alien to the British educational system but which can, and perhaps should, routinely be part of schools' provision. In so doing, there will be an intentional match between principles and practice, for this is the pre-eminent area that links education with the community and the wider society.

The 'ideology' of this chapter explicitly embraces the view that it is the responsibility of teachers, schools and LEAs to ensure that all adults who have care of children and control over them, and responsibilities for their education and welfare, work together for their benefit. The belief system propounded in this chapter eschews exhortation, however, and has a bias towards a presentation of current thinking and work that illuminates and substantiates these views.

Parental involvement is a contemporaneous issue that reverberates in national and local political circles. All the main political parties have, for several years, declared a commitment to increase significantly parental input into decision-making, and advocate an extension of consumer choice into educational spheres. 'Parent power', a phrase used in the media and by politicians, however, refers to different faces of the same coin, depending upon party dogma. The enthusiastic espousal of parental rights by politicians of all shades may be inspired less by genuine conviction than by the fact that there has been a demonstrable and impressive groundswell of action and commitment by 'ordinary' people, parents, governors, teachers and other practitioners. In fact, the complex interplay of these factors is reflected in the philosophy as well as provisions of the Education Reform Act, a theme expanded in this chapter.

Children's special educational needs are best appraised within a whole-school context in which each child has equal, though uniquely differing, access to curriculum and other opportunities offered by the school. Thus, a school that includes parental involvement as part of its provision potentially offers all children on its roll the chance to benefit. Chapter 1 sought to realign practice in primary education with that of remedial/special education, in order to delineate how special educational needs can be met within primary settings. By the same token, this chapter will, in part, explore how recent, identifiable, good practice in parental involvement in primary schools and special education settings can provide models for primary special needs practice.

En route towards the goal of proposing a viable framework within which parents, teachers, and those from other agencies can operate, a number of related issues will also be considered. These include the notions of empowerment, partnership, responsibilities towards the propagation of parental involvement, and, finally, the reality of where schools and their teachers, homes and families are located, in contemporary multicultural communities.

THE ATTITUDES OF TEACHERS AND PARENTS

A certain circularity characterises arguments about parental involvement in schools that are based on partial information. That is to say, how do we know if innovative practice comes about as a function of changed attitudes or whether attitudes are changed as a consequence of trying it out? Can teachers and parents be coerced into co-operative ventures by those with the influence to instigate (head teachers, advisers, educational psychologists, for example) when their conviction and enthusiasm are lacking?

The nature of innovation and the persuasive effects these ventures can have may mask, even obliterate, latent resistance. The information we have to hand as to the extent and enthusiasm of parental involvement can only be partial, since we are describing dynamic forces that are already operational, and so the task of keeping a check upon evolving practice becomes well-nigh impossible. It is difficult to keep an accurate and updated chronicle of initiatives that are taking place all over Britain, and, sometimes, in schools where teachers and parents may be unaware that their work represents a phenomenon of our times.

We can now witness a manifest change in attitude in the existence of many well-maintained parental involvement ventures and smoothly functioning home–school links, whatever the genesis and the original impetus were. Their success buries myths that earlier attitude surveys uncovered concerning parents' perceptions of teachers' inaccessibility and teachers' perceptions of parents' indifference. Views recently expressed have been within contexts of some degree of active and viable parent–teacher co-operation. These are briefly exemplified below, and demonstrate some commonality in views between teachers and parents in mainstream and special education settings. Since views can be held about and expressed on any number of educational issues, only a brief, selective dip will be made into parents' and teachers' views pertinent to the areas discussed in this book.

PARENTS' VIEWS

Some studies on parental involvement in reading (Griffiths and Hamilton, 1984, and see Topping and Wolfendale, 1985) have sought parental views as part of evaluation. Notwithstanding a perhaps predictable halo effect, their attitudes to this particular form of parental involvement with the curriculum have been positive and enthusiastic – they feel that their knowledge of the reading process (teaching and learning) has been enhanced, they are clearer about schools' own methods and goals, they endorse the ways in which they are welcomed into school (Edwards and Redfern, 1988).

Parents' views on the effects of a 'proper' system of home–school links can be graphic and illuminating. The following quotations provide a momentary snapshot into schemes that appear to pulse with the enthusiasm that the involvement generates:

> All that I have said actually conveys the active side of Home and School link and really there is much more underlying. I don't believe a welcoming environment could exist if the staff were not welcoming. . . . 'Links' collective ability to let children be themselves and grow and

let the parents be themselves, is remarkable. (Parent, Telford Home and School Link Project 1977–1984, p. 21)

The scheme has helped me as much as my child. I have met several people. My child seems confident about going to school. (Parent, Milton Keynes Home–School Link Report 1981, p. 25)

(There is also a relevant study by Tizard, Mortimore and Burchell (1981).)

Turning now to the views of parents of children with special needs, those who have been or are in receipt of PORTAGE attest unequivocally to its specific benefits *vis-à-vis* the child's acquisition of skills and developmental progress, as well as to the wider advantages (Jordan and Wolfendale in Cameron, 1986). PORTAGE evaluation studies (Bendall, Smith and Kushlick, 1984) include feedback of 'consumer' views. It is therefore likely that the endorsement of the PORTAGE model (its technology, methodology, structure and multidisciplinary and partner emphases) by parents contributed to the government's explicit backing of PORTAGE via the Education Support Grant to such under-fives home-based intervention for three years until 1991. (See also references in Table 2.1, 'Major areas of parental involvement in the 1970s and 1980s: some examples'.)

Other parental feedback from joint work was reported in Pugh (1981), and chapter 7, 'Parents and special educational needs', in Wolfendale (1983) provides extensive references to successful joint intervention work (pp. 115–19 and see References List B, pp. 127–30).

On the broader front of access to information and support whilst their children are going through assessment procedures, representative parent groups expressed their views to the Warnock Committee (1978, Chapter 9) and to the Select Committee (1987). Both of these major reports on special education contain recommendations for closer working links based in part on parents' views. Indeed the Select Committee explicitly recommended creation of parents' 'befrienders' to help, guide and support parents through the 1981 Education Act assessment (endorsed in Circular 22/89; DES, 1989). Several LEAs have developed a working partnership in this area with local parents' groups (see Phillips, 1989). Still, the mismatch of perceptions uncovered by Sandow and Stafford (1986) continues to be of concern and, despite encouraging developments, procedures to gain access to and heed parents' opinions and feelings need to be established in many places.

TEACHERS' VIEWS

A similar picture is painted in this section. That is, where there are already viable and active forms of parental involvement the benefits are so evident and so clearly outweigh the perceived disadvantages as to be reflected in the positive, enthusiastic attitudes of teachers. Again, this can be exemplified in parental involvement in reading (Griffiths and Hamilton, 1984; Topping and Wolfendale, 1985). Likewise, the attitudes of several hundreds of teachers (headteachers, class teachers, advisory and support teachers, other responsible post-holders) sampled via a face-to-face questionnaire carried out routinely by myself at INSET sessions from 1984 (and which continues) into parental involvement showed a clear connection between a lively amount of parental involvement in schools and a confident belief in its benefits to all concerned.

Winkley (1985) discusses the sources of misperceptions of teachers and parents referred to above and goes on to document the programme of parental involvement in the junior school of which he was headteacher. He captures an evolving situation and changing attitudes in these words:

> schools' relationships with parents develop slowly, artfully, over a period of time, to the point where it virtually becomes a tradition, an unspoken expectation for both teachers and parents to behave in certain ways. . . . new teachers and the parents of new children tend to accept, absorb and develop the tradition. The key factor is that the participants find the time spent worthwhile and enjoyable. (p. 83)

Within the setting of a school for children with moderate learning difficulties, Marra (1984) sets out some of the requisites for successful parent–teacher interaction and a functioning relationship within the school of which he was headteacher. 'Warts and all' are described in the process and he concludes:

> What has been described . . . reflects parental involvement in its infancy; the objective of educational involvement and the goal of partnership have yet to be reached. However, what have been described are some of the principles for a possible partnership based on experience. (p. 145)

That teachers and parents have a great deal in common is an intrinsic part of the rationale of parental involvement programmes, as is spelled out in Topping and Wolfendale (1985) in chapter 1 and summarised in these words: 'This complementarity of "role" is less a neat formula than it is perceived to constitute a framework for cooperative working' (p. 12).

This commonality was explored on a parent–teacher inservice

course described by Davies and Davies (1985), the aim of which was to identify the extent to which these parties agreed and disagreed on certain issues seen as fundamental if the dream of parent–teacher partnership were ever to become a reality. These authors, like Marra, on the basis of this and other experience set out requisites, which, for them, include pre- and inservice training, in part to prevent enthusiastic but hasty adoption of parental involvement schemes that do not rest on carefully thought through systems of planning, execution, management and evaluation. As one model for such planning, in the area of parental involvement in reading, Topping and Wolfendale (1985) put forward one schema (chapter 32). For parental involvement in other curriculum and learning areas, Topping proposed another model (Topping, 1986).

It is likely that under the formalised banner of co-operative ventures, some of the misperceptions, anxieties, defences cited in Dowling and Osborne (1985) are reduced if not eliminated. For example, conjoint problem identification and problem solving can be facilitated. To some extent, parental involvement can be viewed as a 'preventive' approach in that 'problems' can be 'caught' and dealt with before they exacerbate. Reported joint work in this area is rare – later in this chapter there is an outline of practical strategies to bring it about.

Some time has been spent in the preceding discussion on the important issue of attitudes and what it requires for a situation conducive to the promotion of good working relations to be set up. An attempt has been made to weave into the discussion threads from mainstream and special education settings to demonstrate that the requisites are the same and therefore applicable to integrated settings in which special educational needs are being met. Teachers may be expected to have certain knowledge, skills and sensitivities in relation to acute or enduring problems and handicapping conditions. But, within the framework of collective responsibility outlined in Chapter 1, the network of caring and informed personnel to liaise closely with parents becomes more feasible.

PARTNERSHIP BETWEEN SCHOOL AND HOME: THE EXTENT AND THE REALITIES

There have been many well-documented initiatives in parental involvement (Cullingford, 1985; Topping and Wolfendale, 1985; Atkin, Bastiani and Goode, 1988; Macleod, 1989; Wolfendale, 1989, 1992), which collectively provide testimony to the effectiveness of collaboration and which singly demonstrate the potential and the limitations of equality and power sharing. There are signs that some of the work is taking root within schools as part of routine provision. Some schools are even evolving a policy on involving parents that becomes the official imprimatur to ventures that may have started in an *ad hoc*, modest way. That is, some of the realities were tested out prior to formal acceptance at 'policy' level.

Some of the work is multidisciplinary, wherein parents contribute and these ventures are seen as part of a wider network of service provision for meeting special needs which is regarded as cost-effective and egalitarian (McConkey, 1985). PORTAGE, in which parents are the educators and therefore play the central role, is seen as coming the nearest to a model of parental partnership, and even then some would argue that the final power of decision-making (in terms of resource allocation, personnel deployment) is retained by professionals.

There are writers who have cast doubt upon the possibility of 'true' partnership coming about. Potts (1983) sees partnership as tokenism, a kind of window-dressing without parents ever really sharing power. Gliedmann and Roth (1981) are of the view that partnership cannot come about until parents oversee and orchestrate the services that professionals provide for their children. They question the almost 'God-given' self-perception of professionals about the omnipotence of their expertise and aver that

> parents of all races and social classes should be able to pick and choose among different experts, obtain outside opinions when dissatisfied with the services or advice provided by a professional and constantly evaluate the professional's performance in terms of the overall needs of the growing child. (p. 235)

The possibility of this sort of central managerial role within education and child-focused services is also raised by Beattie (1985), who sees the potential of much more direct participation by parents/citizens in power sharing as constituting a challenge to traditional tenets about where power should properly reside and who wields it, including control over the curriculum. This raises questions about the parameters of the governors' role whether they be parents or representing other factions (governors' responsibilities and schools' relationships with their governing bodies in relation to special needs policies and practice are discussed in Chapter 5 of this book).

In order to demonstrate that partnership need not remain an ideal, an aspiration, some writers with firsthand experience of working as practitioners at the 'interface' with parents have attempted definitions of knowledge, skills and experience (Mittler and McConachie, 1983)

Table 2.1 *Major areas of parental involvement in the 1970s and 1980s: some examples*

	Areas of involvement	Key sources
Parents coming in to school	Helping with reading	Griffiths and Hamilton, 1984; Topping and Wolfendale, 1985; Young and Tyre, 1983; Davis and Stubbs, 1988;
	As co-workers in the classroom	Wolfendale, 1983, chs. 3 and 4; Long, 1986; Atkin, Bastiani and Goode, 1988
Parents as educators at home	Parental involvement in reading, language, maths learning and 'homework'	As above, also Topping, 1986; Wolfendale and Bryans, 1986; Merttens and Vass, 1990;
	Parent–teacher workshops	Wolfendale, 1983, ch. 7
	PORTAGE	See below
	Parent education	Pugh and De'Ath, 1984
Home–school links	School reports	Goacher and Reid, 1983
	Written communication (newsletters) in English and community languages	Bastiani, 1989
	Open files	
	Home–school council	Templeton, 1989
	Home visiting	Raven, 1980
Community education/community	Parents' rooms in school	LEAs with Community Education
	Parents and others attending classes in school	
	Multidisciplinary work	Fitzherbert in Cullingford, 1985
	Local and national parents' associations	ACE, CASE
	Parents' support groups	Wolfendale, 1989
	Parent governors	Sallis, 1988
Parents and special needs	Parental involvement in assessment	Wolfendale, 1988; Cunningham and Davis, 1985
	Parental involvement in behaviour and learning programmes	Carr, 1980; Westmacott and Cameron, 1981;
		McConkey, 1985; Mittler and McConachie, 1983; Newson and Hipgrave, 1982;
		Wolfendale, 1983, ch. 7
	PORTAGE	Cameron, 1982; Dessent, 1983; Daly et al., 1985; Copley et al., 1986; Cameron, 1986

'complementary expertise' (Cunningham and Davis, 1985) and 'equivalent expertise' (Wolfendale, 1983).

These are the key operational concepts embedded within an equal dialogue. I have explored how operational these elements can be as, for example, 'equivalent expertise', 'a reciprocal relationship', leading to 'mutual accountability, mutual gain' (Wolfendale, 1983, chapter 2) in an exercise in which parents make an equal contribution to the assessment processes under the 1981 Education Act (Wolfendale, 1988). The transitional, evolving nature of working towards such aims has been expressed by Davie (1985):

> a rational understanding of the dynamic of partnership and collaboration in these terms would not *guarantee* a closer and more effective relationship in working for children, but it might help to structure situations or shift attitudes in ways which could promote progress. (p. 7)

BUILDING UPON EFFECTIVE AND EMERGING PRACTICE WITHIN THE CONTEXT OF THE EDUCATION REFORM ACT

The evolutionary nature of the working relationship between home and school has been spurred and hastened by the advent of the ERA. Embedded in its provisions are a number of key requirements that confer obligations upon schools towards parents and, correspondingly, grant parents specific rights:

- parental choice of school ('open enrolment')
- opportunities to 'opt out' of LEA control (significant voting majority)
- to receive an annual report on their child's progress from school
- to receive curriculum plans for the year
- to know results of assessment, via published school and LEA lists
- to have information on the school and National Curriculum
- school governing bodies have legal responsibility for the National Curriculum, staff hiring and firing, budget (parents represented)

These rights sum to one fundamental right, which is for parents to be involved in education not just as consumer recipients but as active joint decision-makers.

Schools will be able to utilise existing working relationships with parents (see HMI report on parental involvement in schools: 1989–90: HMI, 1991) as a springboard for incorporating the new requirements, and those LEAs which have actively pursued a parental participation policy will doubtless draw upon accumulated expertise to consider how best to deliver to parents in the future.

The kind of initiatives that have been initiated at LEA level, from the early 1980s include: appointment of home–school liaison teachers and advisers; school–home reading schemes; inservice training; preparation of materials; supporting individual school-based programmes.

There are a number of parental involvement initiatives which can be classified as 'emerging' in that they have only been tried out on a small scale or as pilot projects. Each of these ideas, if implemented on a larger scale, would be compatible with existing parental involvement activities, with ERA requirements, and with the spirit of accountability and quality assurance that informs so much of contemporary educational thinking. These ideas include:

- Consulting parents
  There is thought to be considerable mileage in asking parents what they think about their children's schools! The simple premise behind a number of pilot initiatives (Abbott, Birchenaugh and Steadman, 1989) is 'every parent has a positive interest in and expectations of, the school which their child attends' (p. 3). A number of benefits accrue from the exercise of asking parents for their views, as is attested in a case study reported by Hargreaves *et al.* (1989) describing how parents were consulted as part of a secondary school audit of its teaching reading policy and how their views were incorporated into a change of strategy. Abbott *et al.* outline a number of ways of consulting parents.

- Home–school agreement
  There is current discussion on the merits and disadvantages of there being a contractual basis to home–school relations. The idea of a contract as suggested by the National Association of Head Teachers is anathema to many, whereas others perceive a written agreement to be a sensible way of articulating mutual responsibilities towards the children in their charge. One primary school of this author's acquaintance has issued such an agreement, which includes mutual accountabilities such as:
  'School will inform you if there is any cause for concern about your child's social, emotional or academic progress and together we will plan a course of action' (teachers)
  'that if there are any problems in school I will support joint action with the school and work together to overcome difficulties' (parents).
  Such an agreement, or charter even, could offer support and protection if it is approached in a spirit of partnership and not in a formal contractual way. Macbeth (1989) discusses and gives models of such agreements, including his 'signed understanding'.

- Involving parents in assessment: towards a system of reciprocal reporting
  Parental involvement in assessment is a still-burgeoning area, developing its own methodology and practices (Wolfendale, 1987, 1988). Of recent interest has been the parental dimension to school-based assessment, particularly on entry to school (sometimes referred to as 'baseline' assessment). This has given teachers the advantage of a vital and informed perspective (Wolfendale, 1990, 1991) in their task of gathering past and concurrent information about children from a range of sources.

  Schools are now required to report to parents on how their children are progressing in school and with the National Curriculum. They are developing their own formats, which could include incorporation of a record of achievement approach, as suggested by SEAC (1990). The reciprocal reporting model advocated in Wolfendale (1991) could pave the way for effective written and verbal communication between school and home over children's progress.

INVOLVING PARENTS OF CHILDREN WITH SPECIAL NEEDS: A MATTER OF RIGHTS AND ENTITLEMENTS

Many of the existing and emerging initiatives involve children with special educational needs, whether they are in mainstream or in special schools. In fact, notable schemes have been instigated within special needs contexts (cf. PORTAGE), as an earlier book on the topic demonstrated (Pugh, 1981). As was emphasised in Chapter 1, special needs are part of equal opportunities and all children have an inalienable right to all curriculum opportunities.

The same principles must, consistently, be applied to their parents, who must, by way of a moral imperative, be guaranteed fullest expression of their legal rights under all the recent Education Acts (1981, 1986, 1988). This must include opportunities for redress over sensitive matters to do with assessment and placement. Hence the recommendation in Circular 22/89 for befriending systems to be set up (DES, 1989; see above, p. 21). The potential of this idea is being explored in a DES-funded project based at the National Children's Bureau.

A significant 'special needs' development of the 1980s has been the creation of parents' groups; their purpose and activities are chronicled in Wolfendale (1989, ch. 8) and these encompass local and national lobbying, parent-to-parent training and support groups. Cameron and Sturge-Moore (1990) illustrate vividly the realisation of parental empowerment and, basing their argument on the confidence and skills parents have accrued in these endeavours, encourage all parents of children with special needs to act and insist upon their rights and entitlements.

Parents of children with special needs could, understandably, feel that the advent of ERA is a mixed blessing. The positive aspects of this 'balance sheet' comprise entitlement principles, opportunities for a differentiated curriculum and individual programmes of study, statements linked to the National Curriculum, requirement upon schools to keep parents regularly informed of progress. However, these are tempered by uncertainties and concerns over whether or not progress towards integration is facilitated or hampered by LMS, 'opting out' and open enrolment; whether modification of the National Curriculum or disapplication from it will mean marginalising of special needs children; whether SATs will prove to be of little benefit to children with a range of special needs and who could at worst be exposed and vulnerable in a national assessment system. Parents' groups will have plenty on their agendas for some time to come.

IMPLEMENTING A SCHOOL-BASED POLICY ON PARENTAL PARTICIPATION

The many elements that go to make a comprehensive parental involvement programme are presented in Figure 2.1 in the form of a wheel. The purpose behind this form of representation is to:

1. Demonstrate the intimate connections between the school, the home, and the community – indeed, the 'reciprocal' nature of the interaction.
2. Make the point to readers that in most schools some form of parental contact and involvement has been well established over a number of years.
3. Reiterate that this represents a comprehensive programme, possibly goals towards which schools might work.
4. Illustrate how policy, practice and provision on special needs can be incorporated into general parental involvement structures.

Each of the activities on the spoke of the wheel has been tried out in British schools, even though there is probably no one school that includes all the elements in a concurrent programme of parental involvement. A number of texts give suggestions for practical implementation of many of these ideas (McConkey, 1985; Long,

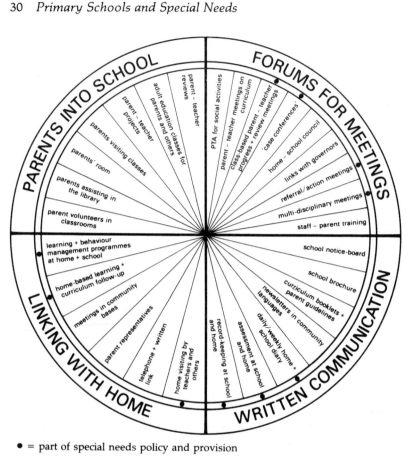

● = part of special needs policy and provision

Figure 2.1 The wheel: a programme of parental involvement

1986; Sullivan, 1988), while Bastiani (1989) outlines a whole-school approach and Stacey (1991) considers the working relationship between parents and teachers within a whole-school policy context.

It is proposed that primary school staff, in conjunction with parents and other support staff, formulate a threefold plan of action to involve:

1. reviewing existing parental involvement
2. reviewing current policy and provision on special educational needs (see Chapter 7)
3. reformulating parental involvement to incorporate special educational needs.

This may necessitate devising a goal plan and setting out a timetable for achieving short and longer-term goals.

As can be seen, the wheel includes some elements that can routinely be part of parental involvement yet could also be applicable to working with parents of children with acknowledged special educational needs as and when this is appropriate. To effect these working links in practice involves making 1 + 2 (above) equal to 3. Thus, from summing 1 + 2, it is possible to abstract these elements from those activities which are denoted on the wheel:

- noting and sharing concerns
- referral
- assessment
- action and intervention
- recording
- review

Each of these 'special needs' *vis-à-vis* parental involvement will be picked up and pursued in the relevant chapters of this book. The elements are finally seen to cohere once more in Chapter 7.

The following list summarises the possibilities of participation by parents at a number of levels.

- monitoring progress and receiving reports;
- helping their own child in school;
- working with school staff to develop an individual learning programme for their child;
- involvement with their child in paired or shared reading or other educational programmes;
- receiving home visits by teachers aimed at establishing links over individual children or to work on difficulties

In the school's educational process:

- discussions about the curriculum;
- involvement in the development of particular educational programmes, e.g. shared reading, maths, programmes for multi-ethnic education;
- parents helping in the classroom, e.g. hearing readers, helping with groups or project work;
- providing special interest topics;
- parent workshops on teaching or other school developments

In school management and policy making:

- involvement in development of school policy through consultation (e.g. parent surveys) and parent representation (e.g. on the school's governing body);

- parents forming pressure groups to lobby the local authority for resources, or to prevent mergers/closures/reorganisations;
- involvement in decisions relating to government legislation, beyond that required through parent governors

It is worth noting that the new requirements imposed by ERA and already cited, pose new challenge to schools. If, in the future they are to be judged by a number of performance indicators (Fitz-Gibbon, 1990), the degree and quality of home–school activities are obvious candidates for inclusion on a list of performance indicators. The activities set out on the wheel in Figure 2.1 and the levels of involvement postulated above could serve as markers for determining such indicators.

SCHOOL IN THE COMMUNITY

It was announced at the outset of this chapter that there would be an explicit commitment to the involvement of parents in their children's development and education. The rationales for this stance have been more fully discussed elsewhere (Wolfendale, 1983; McConachie, 1986b) and the chapter abounds with references to research and practice in this area.

The ecological perspective has always been central to these rationales (Bronfenbrenner, 1979) and there are those who, like this author, aver that it is more or less axiomatic that parental involvement is synonymous with an approach that sees school as being centrally part of the child's world, along with home, family, peers, friends, social institutions, and the neighbourhood. Writers like Apter (1982) perceive the 'problems' of children not so much as 'within-child' problems as problems within these wider systems. The moves towards parental participation/partnership and community education exemplify ecological principles in practice.

It is imperative now, within a multicultural society (Tomlinson, 1984; Swann Report, 1985) that can no longer lay claim to monotheistic religious practice, to incorporate into schooling cultural perspectives and customs that reflect pluralist practice. A schism between home and school is no longer tenable in our communities where there is more than one neighbourhood language, where shops sell produce from all over the world, where dress reflects cultural diversity. Young children are entitled, as they grow up, to feel that there is a rapprochement between home and school and that their teachers and parents share common goals on their behalf.

REFERENCES

Abbott, R., Birchenaugh, M. and Steadman, S. (1989) *External Perspectives in School-based Review.* York: Longman.

Apter, S. (1982) *Troubled Children, Troubled Systems.* Oxford: Pergamon.

Atkin, J., Bastiani, J. and Goode, J. (1988) *Listening to Parents.* London: Croom Helm.

Bastiani, J. (1989) *Working with Parents: A Whole-school Approach.* Windsor: NFER-Nelson.

Beattie, N. (1985) *Professional Parents.* Lewes: Falmer Press.

Bendall, S., Smith, J. and Kushlick, A. (1984) *National Study of Portage-type Home Teaching Services: A Research Report,* no. 162. Health Care Evaluation Research Team, University of Southampton, 45/47 Salisbury Road, Highfield, Southampton, Hants.

Bowers, T. (ed.) (1984) *Management and the Special School.* London: Croom Helm.

Bronfenbrenner, U. (1979) *The Ecology of Human Development: Experiments by Nature and Design.* Cambridge, MA: Harvard University Press.

Cameron, J. and Sturge-Moore, L. (1990) *Ordinary, Everyday Families: A Human Rights Issue.* Mencap London Division, 115 Golden Lane, London EC1Y 0TJ.

Cameron, R.J. (ed.) (1982) *Working Together: Portage in the UK.* Windsor: NFER-Nelson.

Cameron, R.J. (ed.) (1986) *Portage, Parents and Professionals: Helping Families with Special Needs.* Windsor: NFER-Nelson.

Carr, J. (1980) *Helping Your Handicapped Child.* Harmondsworth: Penguin.

Copley, M., Bishop, M. and Porter, J. (eds) (1986) *Portage: More than a Teaching Programme.* Windsor: NFER-Nelson.

Cullingford, C. (ed.) (1985) *Parents, Teachers and Schools.* London: Robert Royce.

Cunningham, C. and Davis, H. (1985) *Working with Parents.* Milton Keynes: Open University Press.

Daly, B., Addington, J., Kerfoot, S. and Sigston, A. (eds) (1985) *Portage: The Importance of Parents.* Windsor: NFER-Nelson.

Davie, R. (1985) *Equalities and Inequalities in Working Together for Children, in Partnership with Parents: A Contrast in Stress,* Partnership Paper No. 6. National Children's Bureau, 8 Wakley Street, London EC1V 7QE.

Davies, J. D. and Davies, P. A. 'Parents, teachers and children with special needs'. In Cullingford, op. cit., ch. 7.

Davis, C. and Stubbs, R. (1988) *Shared Reading in Practice.* Milton Keynes: Open University Press.

DES (1989) *Assessments and Statements of Special Educational Needs: Procedures within the Education, Health and Social Services,* Circular 22/89. London: DES.

Dessent, T. (ed.) (1983) *What Is Important about Portage?* Windsor: NFER-Nelson.

Dowling, E. and Osborne, E. (eds) (1985) *The Family and the School: A Joint Systems Approach to Working with Children.* London: Routledge & Kegan Paul.

Edwards, V. and Redfern, A. (1988) *At Home in School: Parent Participation in Primary Education*. London: Routledge.

Fitz-Gibbon, C. (ed.) (1990) *Performance Indicators*, BERA Dialogues No. 2. Clevedon: Multilingual Matters.

Gliedmann, J. and Roth, W. (1981) 'Parents and professionals'. In Swann, W. (ed.) *The Practice of Special Education*. Oxford: Basil Blackwell/Open University Press.

Goacher, B. and Reid, M. (1983) *School Reports to Parents*. Windsor: NFER-Nelson.

Griffiths, A. and Hamilton, D. (1984) *Parent, Teacher, Child*. London: Methuen.

Hargreaves, D., Hopkins, D., Leask, M., Connolly, J. and Robinson, P. (1989) *Planning for School Development: Advice to Governors, Headteachers and Teachers*. London: DES/HMSO.

Harris, J. (ed.) (1986) *Child Psychology in Action: Linking Research and Practice*. Beckenham: Croom Helm.

HMI (1991) *Parents and Schools: Aspects of Parental Involvement in Primary and Secondary Schools 1989-1990*. London: HMSO.

Long, R. (1986) *Parental Involvement in Primary Schools*. Basingstoke: Macmillan.

Macbeth, A. (1989) *Involving Parents: Effective Parent–Teacher Relations*. Oxford: Heinemann Educational.

McConachie, H. (1986a) *Parents and Mentally Handicapped Children: A Review of Research Issues*. Beckenham: Croom Helm.

McConachie, H. (1986b) 'Parents' contribution to the education of their child'. In Coupe, J. and Porter, J. (eds) *The Education of Children with Severe Learning Difficulties: Bridging the Gap between Research and Practice*, ch. 10. Beckenham: Croom Helm.

McConkey, R. (1985) *Working with Parents: A Practical Guide for Teachers and Therapists*. Beckenham: Croom Helm.

Macleod, F. (ed.) (1989) *Parents and Schools: The Contemporary Challenge*. Lewes: Falmer Press.

Marra, M. (1984). 'Parents of children with moderate learning difficulties'. In Bowers, op. cit.

Merttens, R. and Vass, J. (1990) *Bringing School Home: Children and Parents Learning Together*. London: Hodder & Stoughton.

Milton Keynes Home–School Link Report (1981).

Mittler, P. and McConachie, H. (eds) (1983) *Parents, Professionals and Mentally Handicapped People*. London: Croom Helm.

Newson, E. and Hipgrave, T. (1982) *Getting Through to Your Handicapped Child*. Cambridge: Cambridge University Press.

Phillips, R. (1989) 'The Newham Parents' Centre'. In Wolfendale, S., op. cit., ch. 7.

Plowden, B. (Chair) (1967) *Children and Their Primary Schools*. London: HMSO.

Potts, P. (1983) 'What difference would integration make to the professionals?' In Booth, T. and Potts, P. (eds) *Integrating Special Education*. Oxford: Basil Blackwell.

Pugh, G. (1981) *Parents as Partners*. London: National Children's Bureau.
Pugh, G. and De'Ath, E. (1984) *The Needs of Parents*. Basingstoke: Macmillan.
Raven, J. (1980) *Parents, Teachers and Children: A Study of an Educational Home Visiting Scheme*. Sevenoaks: Hodder & Stoughton/Scottish Council for Research in Education.
Sallis, J. (1988) *Schools, Parents and Governors: A New Approach to Accountability*. London: Routledge.
Sandow, S. and Stafford, P. (1986) Parental perceptions and the 1981 Education Act. *British Journal of Special Education* 13 (1) March 19–21.
SEAC (1990) *Records of Achievement in Primary Schools*, London: School Examinations and Assessment Council, Newcombe House, 45 Notting Hill Gate, London W11 3JB.
Select Committee (1987) *Report on the 1981 Education Act*, Vol. 1. London: HMSO.
Stacey, M. (1991) *Parents and Children Together: Partnership in Primary and Nursery Education*. Milton Keynes: Open University Press.
Sullivan, M. (1988) *Parents and Schools*. Leamington Spa: Scholastic Publications.
Swann, M. (Chair) (1985) *Education for All*. Report of the Committee of Enquiry into the education of children from ethnic minority groups. London: HMSO.
Telford (Shropshire) Home and School Link Project (1977–1984).
Templeton, J. (1989) 'Creation of a home–school council in a secondary school'. In Wolfendale, op. cit., ch. 5.
Tizard, B., Mortimore, J. and Burchell, B. (1981) *Involving Parents in Nursery and Infant Schools*. London: Grant McIntyre.
Tomlinson, S. (1984) *Home and School in Multicultural Britain*. London: Batsford.
Topping, K. (1986) *Parents as Educators*. Beckenham: Croom Helm.
Topping, K. and Wolfendale, S. (eds) (1985) *Parental Involvement in Children's Reading*. Beckenham: Croom Helm.
Warnock, M. (Chair) (1978) *Special Educational Needs*. London: HMSO.
Westmacott, E. V. S. and Cameron, R. J. (1981) *Behaviour Can Change*. Basingstoke: Macmillan.
Winkley, D, 'The school's view of parents'. In Cullingford, op. cit., ch. 5.
Wolfendale, S. (1983) *Parental Participation in Children's Development and Education*. New York and London: Gordon & Breach.
Wolfendale, S. (1987) The evaluation and revision of the ALL ABOUT ME pre-school parent-completed scales. *Early Child Development and Care* 29, 473–558.
Wolfendale, S. (1988) *The Parental Contribution to Assessment*. Developing Horizons No. 10. Stratford-upon-Avon: National Council for Special Education.
Wolfendale, S. (ed.) (1989) *Parental Involvement: Developing Networks between School, Home and Community*. London: Cassell.
Wolfendale, S. (1990) *ALL ABOUT ME*. Nottingham Educational Supplies, Ludlow Hill Road, West Bridgeford, Nottingham.
Wolfendale, S. (1991) 'Parents and teachers working together on the

assessment of children's progress'. In Lindsay, G. and Miller, A. (eds) *Psychological Services for Primary Schools*. York: Longman.

Wolfendale, S. (1992) *Empowering Parents and Teachers: Working for Children*. London: Cassell.

Wolfendale, S. and Bryans, T. (1986) *WORD PLAY: Language Activities for Young Children and their Parents*. Stafford: National Association for Remedial Education.

Young, P. and Tyre, P. (1983) *Dyslexia or Illiteracy: Realising the Right to Read*. Milton Keynes: Open University Press.

Planning and managing learning

Teachers have a juggling act to perform; they are encouraged to recognise the special needs of all children in their charge, and urged at the same time to be alert and sensitive to individual needs.

It is possible that the notion of learning difficulties and deficit models arose in part from teachers' need to manage their classrooms and that to posit a separate 'breed' of children with learning and behaviour difficulties helped them to organise the mainstream of the classroom, and enabled them, with justification, to call upon remedial teachers to help with the harder-to-teach children.

At the heart of this book lies the philosophy that *all* children have individual needs in learning and other ways, but that the teaching force in any one school can, corporately, manage classrooms and school provision to meet those individual needs. The rhetoric goes beyond calling for attitude change to the reality of setting out teaching and management objectives to facilitate the planning of learning climates within schools.

SCHOOL AS A CENTRE FOR LEARNING

Children's, and indeed adults', learning takes place anywhere, everywhere, at any time. School-based learning, as it has evolved, is characterised by direction, intention, the provision of tools to assist learning, and the concentration in one setting of adult expertise to facilitate, by formalised means, knowledge and skill acquisition.

Our thinking has evolved over the time-span of this century, from a view of school as a place which promoted rote learning, via drill, to a view which encompasses a plurality of methods and richness of curriculum, set within far broader perspectives. For instance, the aims of education as discussed by Hirst and Peters (1970) would simply not have been thought about, let alone acted upon, at the turn of the century when class chanting of reading primers was common and children who did not keep up the pace fell by the wayside. Economic factors had primacy over consideration of the education of the whole child.

Contemporary teachers have the central aspiration of aiming to reach and teach each child in their classes, assisting each one to attain his or her potential. However, up to now, there has not been an obligation upon schools to demonstrate their approaches *vis-à-vis* individual children, and the accountability system, whereby schools have to explain and justify progress and lack of progress, has only just begun.

The formulation of a National Curriculum, which schools and governing bodies now have to deliver 'efficiently', is the major intended vehicle for such accountability. The monitoring process comes via tracking children's progress through their attainment targets and programmes of study and from SATs results.

The issue of progress of children with any kind of learning difficulty or special need that could halt progress with learning unless met is starkly highlighted, even exposed, within this tight specification. For these accountability procedures to ensure higher standards in education run the risk of potentially failing any so-called minority of pupils by targeting the majority. So it is vital that educationalists make the most of the opportunities to use the National Curriculum and assessment arrangements on behalf of children with special needs to ensure that they do not become the forgotten minority and that the provisions for individualising the curriculum are built into each class learning programme.

These prefatory remarks are intended as the backcloth to this chapter, which adopts a problem-solving approach to learning; that is, children's rate and pace of learning can be observed (process) and what they have 'learned' (e.g. facts, reasoning competence, specific skills) can be measured (product). Learning, for all of us, takes place by means of a mix of approaches or strategies, e.g. trial, error self-correction, rehearsal, repetition of acts, rote learning, and so on. Our strategies can be viewed as composites of problem-solving devices to assist the learning process, to overcome learning hurdles ('getting stuck', plateauing, needing more opportunity and exposure, practice, etc.).

'Learning difficulties' therefore can be conceptualised as something all adults can experience at any point in acquiring facts or new skills (changing the wheel of a car, mending a watch, memorising the itinerary of a touring holiday). This analogy with adult learning is a deliberate reminder that learning is a continuous and continuing process and we start to employ our problem-solving strategies very early on as young children.

The pedagogic responsibilities of teachers and others in education are to enable and assist children to:

- understand the point and purpose of the learning tasks presented to them and in which they engage
- learn how to learn
- evolve effective learning strategies
- identify learning hurdles, 'sticking-points' along the way and apply appropriate problem-solving learning strategies.

The direct and conscious involvement of all children in their own learning has not been a feature of primary schools. So many children who experience some learning blockage have not traditionally been enabled to identify the source of their difficulty at an early enough point in time to want to take action, to co-operate with others acting on their behalf. If early precursors to later learning failure could be identified and acted upon much earlier, a significant number of potential later referrals could be avoided. Indeed, the whole screening 'movement' (Bullock, 1975; Wolfendale and Bryans, 1979) was reliant on the view, itself based on plenty of 'case' and survey evidence, that early identification of early-appearing learning difficulties linked to intervention was a justifiable preventive approach.

Indeed, since the exploratory earlier days of screening, in the mid-1970s, methods of identification linked with setting curriculum objectives and good planning have become more sharply focused and closely targeted, and methods of evaluation are more refined. Some of these approaches will be discussed later in the chapter.

Wolfendale and Bryans (1980) explored some of these 'prereferral' aspects of learning difficulty. We identified them as being subtle, not always noticeable, but accruing signs of temporal difficulties with learning material (e.g. beyond the child's present skill level, too demanding in amount, unclear in presentation and explanation by teacher, totally missing owing to the child's absence from school during a key lesson, etc.). Concomitant with these difficulties were early, again subtle, signs of learning-associated stress, lowered morale ('can't cope') and reduced motivation ('won't try to'). The small-scale intervention project we carried out enabled us to observe and record, first-hand, the performance and responses of a small group of six- to seven-year-old children who had been identified by their teachers (using the Croydon Checklist as an early school progress guide) as showing early-appearing learning difficulties. We felt that irrespective of 'ability', which we decided it was not relevant to assess, the children in question could be enabled to overcome their embryonic difficulties and be assisted to develop appropriate learning strategies and maintain learning motivation.

In the words of Fish (1985), to view all children as having a right to receive learning experiences enabling them to reach their potential 'stretches the concepts of learning and teaching far beyond the basic skills of literacy and numeracy . . . it redefines education as any systematic intervention provided to enhance personal growth and development' (p. 12).

Whether or not some children are 'slow learners', have sensory or physical handicaps that preclude the adoption of some of the more usual methods of information and skill acquisition, the starting point of curriculum planning is each child's 'teachable self', and the formulation of a learning profile that identifies learning assets and locates learning strategies. The chapter aims to represent a mix of practice within theoretical and conceptual frameworks, and, as such, aims to herald the more specific areas that are the subjects of the other books in this primary series (especially Montgomery, 1990).

From the principles can be derived a learning formula applicable uniquely to each child, a theorem that has to be proved in practice, a process that could be facilitated by the National Curriculum structures.

CHANGE AND TRANSITION

A government report on education can be regarded as a marker for future practice in that it presents a comprehensive picture of what the report defines as existing good practice, and, so doing, validates that practice.

So it is with the Warnock Report, which has been credited with being pace-setting and a beacon for special education practice (Welton, Wedell and Vorhaus, 1982). Certainly, the models of integration, inter-agency co-operation and parental involvement considered by Warnock are, with justification, used as markers. Some of the practice the Committee referred to was already manifest but not then widespread. Specifically, in terms of learning and, more particularly, learning difficulties, this related to moves away from IQ testing and towards early identification, curriculum-based assessment, and broadening the role and function of remedial teachers to encompass a special needs brief.

The metamorphosis of remedial teachers from an amateurish, low-status adjunct within schools (this author has been, at various stages, a remedial teacher) into a better organised corps of professionals with clearer, wider terms of reference is one of the phenomena within changing special education.

These developments have been chronicled (Gains and McNicholas, 1979; Brennan, 1982; Gulliford, 1985; Smith, 1985). For instance, the recommendation in Warnock to abolish the distinction between remedial and special education was translated in many LEAs into the appointment of an adviser for special needs, with the all-encompassing brief to unite what passed for remedial and special educational provision under one banner. Likewise, an increasing number of LEAs strengthened the links between special and mainstream schools, and explored how remedial/special teachers can most effectively work with mainstream staff. Those LEAs with an avowed programme of working towards integrated provision incorporated into their blueprints a definite and key place for their cohorts of ex-remedial, now turned 'special needs teaching and advisory', personnel.

Attention will now turn to several key aspects of planning learning and responding to children's learning hurdles that are the proper province within primary schools of a combination of class and advisory teachers in co-operation with other staff, parents and support services (see Chapter 5). First, however, some reference will be made to the concept of learning difficulties, as this has been so influential in guiding the development of services and directing the deployment of personnel.

LEARNING DIFFICULTIES: A REAPPRAISAL

There is an inevitable focus on 'learning difficulties' in the bulk of this chapter, with the broader, more positive perspectives on learning considered towards the end. The emphasis on difficulties to the exclusion of contexts of and conditions for learning has contributed to the separatist traditions already noted and the divisions made between children with learning problems and those without.

Concepts of learning difficulties continue to vex all of us in education. In the United Kingdom the term 'specific learning difficulties' is not uniformly acceptable (and especially with its connotation of if not synonymity with dyslexia, see Farnham-Diggory, 1978) and in fact regarded with ambivalence (Tansley and Pankhurst, 1981).

The official definition of learning difficulties in the Education Act 1981 with its reference to norm yardsticks does little to clarify how the concept could be put into operation (Wedell, 1983). Gulliford (1985) provides a chapter that aims to clarify and explore the types and relativities of learning difficulties. Earlier, I sought to elicit first-hand definitions by teachers themselves of the term, and received responses from 60 teachers of all age-groups. These responses confirmed that there is a wide variety in viewpoint, description and explanation, ranging from:

- *performance deficit* 'inability to concentrate for any length of time, poor memory, lack of co-ordination' (junior class teacher); 'slowness in acquiring knowledge' (infant school maths responsibility)
- *mix of deficit and home circumstances* 'inability to listen and concentrate for any length of time, combined with a lack of parental interest in what the child does in school' (junior class teacher); 'poor motivation because of emotional or behavioural problems or deprived home circumstance' (secondary teacher);

Some mentioned 'lack of ability', which Stott (1978) criticised for the equation of intelligence with learning ability. Very few referred to teaching or school-based factors. So, from practitioners to researchers and theorists, it does seem that there is no standard or generally accepted concept of learning difficulties, but rather a use of the term that is essentially pragmatic: 'a response to perceived needs and an expedient means for allocating resources on a locally agreed priority basis'. The term, then, provides blanket coverage for underachievement and for 'slow' learners (cf. Gulliford, 1985, chapter 3 for categories of mild, moderate, severe, and specific learning difficulties).

This book extends its use to include the lack of any match between a child's learning needs and teaching/learning opportunities to meet these needs. The needs may become 'special' if a disability in one or more areas handicaps a child's efficient learning and she or he has to be enabled to utilise other media, for example:

- a visual disability could call for use of auditory and tactile means (use of other senses)
- a hearing impairment could call for the use of non-verbal communication, signing systems
- a physical disability could call for the use of technological or other aids, like computers.

RESPONDING TO LEARNING DIFFICULTIES: WITH REFERENCE TO BEHAVIOURAL FRAMEWORKS

There are well-documented accounts of attitudes and provision in the United Kingdom from the 1950s on learning difficulties in mainstream schools that have concentrated in the main on slow progress with the basic subjects (Tansley and Gulliford, 1960; McCreesh and Maher, 1974). Considerable expertise in these mainly remedial approaches was built up and paved the way for the 'newer' approaches of the early 1970s in identifying and assessing children's early-appearing learning difficulties (Wolfendale and Bryans, 1979). In turn, the requisites identified by these and other authors (Stott, 1978) led to contemporary developments, characterised as 'teaching by objectives' and 'curriculum-based assessment', which, in general, are grounded in theories of behavioural psychology and represent the application in educational settings of these theoretical frameworks. The work of Ainscow, Tweddle and their colleagues, which was first described in their book (Ainscow and Tweddle, 1979), has generated widespread application of their ideas and a considerable number of further developments. Their work, targeted mainly to children with learning difficulties in mainstream or schools for children with moderate learning difficulties, has been paralleled by similarly behaviourally based approaches for children with severe learning difficulties, e.g. PORTAGE (Bishop, Copley and Porter, 1986; see NFER-Nelson catalogue for the others in the PORTAGE series) and the Education of the Developmentally Young (EDY; McBrien, 1981).

The basic tenets of these approaches are that they:

- obviate any need for psychometric assessment when an inherent, prime purpose is to probe and pin-point precisely a child's task performance in relation to the curriculum areas on which he or she is currently working
- provide opportunities for teachers who know a child best to record his or her current mastery as a basis for planning the next stages
- promote, via their techniques, the idea of positive intervention with a child's learning rather than the deficit model with its undue emphasis on a child's failure
- encourage the notion that the assessment through teaching model is applicable to the broader curriculum than just with the basic subjects (see below).

The publication edited by Wheldall (1981) comprised one of the first compendia of current British work and Jewell and Feiler (1985) provide a useful and succinct review of these approaches and describe their growing adoption (Solity and Bull, 1987).

Ainscow and Tweddle went on to produce a second book (1984), which represents an extension of the work described in their first, and which was developed over a period of seveal years of classroom trials. The materials consist of 122 carefully selected and precisely stated teaching objectives in arithmetic, handwriting, independence (or self-help) skills, language, motor skills, reading, and spelling. In effect the book comprises a nursery, infant, and beginning junior curriculum.

Direct Instruction is another curriculum/method approach (SRA, 1985). Solity (1984) outlines the behavioural principles from which the teaching practice is derived. Whilst DI is associated with being a successful programme within the American Head Start and Follow-Through initiatives (Becker *et al.*, 1981), it is intended for all learners and its curricula include reading, arithmetic and mathematics, language, and spelling from ages 6 to 15 years. In the realms of moderate and severe learning difficulties, Raymond (1984) offers programmes based on teaching by objectives and covering communication, self-help, independence skills, and cognitive tasks, as does Kiernan (1981).

A way of measuring learning that is part of the behavioural 'technology' and that complements the methods and content of learning programmes is precision teaching (Solity and Bull, 1987; Jewell and Feiler, 1985). Precision teaching is not a method of teaching, but rather a way of trying to find out 'what teaches best' by providing daily feedback on the effectiveness of instruction, and by providing techniques for direct and daily measurement, charting and evaluation of individual pupils' progress towards mastering of specific educational tasks (Raybould and Solity, 1985).

The cornerstone of these approaches is the individual education programme. DATAPAC (Daily Teaching and Assessment for Primary Age Children; Akerman *et al.*, 1983) is regarded as an assessment through teaching approach for individual children. This 'package' contains assessment materials (use of 'placement' tests), teaching sheets and teaching instructions covering mathematics, reading, handwriting and spelling.

It has been found to be cost-effective to direct inservice training on these behavioural approaches to groups of teachers within a school, or at a centre, using a dissemination model. An earlier example of the target teacher dissemination model is that of the LEA-backed Croydon Screening Procedures (Wolfendale and Bryans, 1979). Other LEAs have followed suit in adopting a global LEA-backed initiative that aims, in the first instance, simultaneously to reach a number of teachers. A well-known example, and one that has inspired derivatives, is the Coventry SNAP (Special Needs Action Programme; Ainscow and Muncey, 1983, 1984). This combines the production of written materials with inservice back-up and support.

CURRICULUM APPLICATION OF BEHAVIOURAL FRAMEWORKS

Older-style remediation concentrated in the main on reading and literacy skills, and to a much lesser extent on other major curriculum areas. Behavioural programmes have the flexibility to be subject-focused where appropriate (e.g. DATAPAC spelling, DISTAR language or maths) and also broader-based (multiple-subject or related skills areas, e.g. self-help skills, as included within PORTAGE; also see Raymond, 1984). Furthermore, conventional remedial approaches relied on pre- and post-assessment of children's attainment as measures of progress. But the hallmark of the programmes described above is that assessment is intrinsically part of teaching and is therefore continuous measurement, being inbuilt and not grafted onto either end of teaching–learning sequences (Tweddle and Pearson, 1984).

There is an intentional interplay between an individual education programme and broader-based curriculum planning and curriculum management, in terms of an objectives approach. Cameron (1981) and Lister and Cameron (1986) present the rationale for applying objectives to curriculum planning and draw attention to the requirements of the 1981 Education Act for children assessed under the Act to have 'the protection of a statement' (see Chapter 5). A 'good' statement is one that sets out a child's special (learning and other) needs in detail on the basis of comprehensive educational, psychological, medical, and other assessment, and then goes on to specify exactly how these needs can and should be met. Now of course the statement has to be related to the National Curriculum.

Lister and Cameron relate this to schools' contexts in these words: 'objectives for children with special needs should therefore be formulated with reference to the school's overall goals' (p. 7). They then go on to give a quotation from White and Haring (1980) that sums up the child–curriculum equation:

> We cannot begin to individualise an educational program for a child in a vacuum – we need a larger perspective than any single child . . . these expectations take the form of a basic curriculum which translates the school's 'mission' into more specific goals and even more specific objectives which the children are to master at each level in their progress through the school.

Within this model, there is the leeway to progress from very broad teacher management objectives and then onto the specification of a task and attribute analysis.

The sheer specificity of learning programmes, grounded in behavioural principles, set within broader, longer-term curriculum goals, is consistent with the theme of this chapter, that is, the dictates of the curriculum are secondary to the pivotal claims of each child's learning requirements.

CRITIQUES OF BEHAVIOURAL APPROACHES

Lister and Cameron themselves pay some attention to criticisms and possible pitfalls of a curriculum by objectives approach. Critics peering into behavioural domains have been deadlier in their indictments. For example, Strivens (1981) views behaviour modification (which is related to, indeed is a progenitor of, some approaches currently in use and described above) as socially controlling and limiting upon personal autonomy. Thomas (1985) criticises behavioural approaches as not being sufficiently 'context sensitive', whilst Swann (1985) points to the lack of relevance to children's experience outside school of the content of Direct Instruction and DI-derived programmes.

To the charges that behaviour modification and teaching by objectives are but benign forms of social control and put restraints on access to other richer sources of experience, a commentary on the applicability of behaviour approaches within the context of this book seems necessary.

Specifying curriculum goals and learning targets is quite consistent with an ecological approach. Paired reading (Topping and Wolfendale, 1985) and PORTAGE exemplify how a specific technique with its own 'rules' can be applied within and out of school contexts). Children's progress is manifest, generalisable, and rewarding to child, teachers, parents, family; 'control' of the curriculum can be demonstrably shared in school and with family/community settings; skills can be shared and pooled (as the principles are not arcane and mysterious, the psychology within them can be readily given away); far from legitimating social control processes (an oft-repeated critics' cry), the curriculum and educational processes are opened up and the content and teaching methods made accountable to all.

BEHAVIOURAL APPROACHES AND THE NATIONAL CURRICULUM

The conception outlined just above of behavioural approaches is compatible with the behavioural interactionist perspective promoted by Wheldall and Glynn (1989). This book is somewhat of a marker in behavioural history in going further than earlier behavioural orthodoxy to explicitly embrace context and encourage 'initiation by the learner' (p. 23), though Norwich (1990) still feels that learner analysis is the least attended to feature of behavioural approaches. The Learning Profile approach described below epitomises the learner-focused perspective advocated within a generally behavioural framework.

To what extent does the National Curriculum reflect behaviourist approaches and why is this a relevant question to ask, on behalf of children with special needs?

Regarding the second question, the relevance lies in the fact that, as chronicled above, a substantial amount of work has gone into the production and use of behavioural methods to encourage learning and specifically to meet the needs of pupils with learning difficulties. We need to appraise the extent to which such work still stands and can serve as a foundation for National Curriculum-related programme planning in special needs.

A number of texts and packs have appeared that bridge the National Curriculum and special needs and use terminology that is current within behavioural frameworks, such as 'task analysis', 'step to target' (SNIPP, 1990; Webster and Webster, 1990; Lewis, 1991). The ideas of objectives, structure, sequence, progression, differentiation, and so on are already familiar to those advisory teachers and educational psychologists who have worked within instructional approaches. The place of behavioural approaches is likely to be secured with the arrival of the National Curriculum, albeit in adapted forms as befits contemporary thinking on classroom (see Chapter 5) and the pupil perspective (see below).

THE LEARNING PROFILE

The idea and definition of a learning profile was introduced in Chapter 1 and referred to earlier in this chapter. The formulation rests on the assumption that it is the learning assets of a child as well as learning hurdles that are to be assessed by key personnel and that the outcomes will be used to agree on longer-term goals and shorter-term targets right across the curriculum. The learning profile is the first core part of an individual education programme and stands as a reference point for appraisal and review.

The potential of a learning profile was first tentatively explored during 1979 and 1980 (Wolfendale and Bryans, 1980). We constructed learning profiles on each of six children at the end of a 72-session-long (spanning two terms) language-based/small-group intervention programme. We conceptualised the profiles into four parts that, as a whole, we thought could be used as a basis for forward planning. The four sections are:

1. Specific difficulties with learning.
2. Positive features of learning.

3. Learning needs.
4. Trends (documented during and summarised at the end of the intervention programme).

Examples of completed profiles are given in Wolfendale and Bryans (1980). One, of Kenny, entitled 'Profile Analysis', is reproduced in Appendix 1. Although at an embryonic stage of development, Kenny's learning profile shows the potential of its use at initial assessment-recording stage as well as its continuing use, at monitoring and review stages. Appendix 1 also contains a copy of notes 'accompanying the use of profile analysis'; these provide the conceptual background and rationale, give guidelines as to its use and contain extracts from two child profiles drawn up from the intervention project (Wolfendale and Bryans, 1980). As can be seen, the learning profile is intended to be applicable to any intervention, teaching by objectives, or other programme approach.

CONTRIBUTING TO A LEARNING PROFILE: TAKING COLLECTIVE ACTION

In illustrating a collective approach, the key personnel referred to above will, for the purposes of this chapter, be seen to be class teacher, advisory/support/special needs co-ordinator, parent, possibly attached educational psychologist, and, where possible, children themselves. Naturally for some children, other people will be involved and will be identifiably part of the network of provision and support. Examples of this will be given later.

Key tasks will be identified, agreed and shared. The learning profile will be initially drawn up based on the contribution of key people; for example, the profile of Kenny shows how parents' views were incorporated.

The various components that contribute to the learning profile (which is a continuous means of recording, analysing, planning) are presented sequentially in Table 3.1, in chart form where appropriate, giving examples of possible inputs. A key reference list is provided for readers who wish to follow up and implement these various strategies. All the references in these sections have a practical basis (contain plenty of suggestions for assessment and intervention for all learners, irrespective of 'special' needs) or have practical implication for classroom activity. They are asterisked in the reference list at the end of this chapter for readers who wish to follow them up for designing and carrying out practical work.

Other components of a learning profile, such as record-keeping and

Table 3.1 Assessment: options for key people

References key	Class teacher	Support/advisory teacher	Educational psychologist	Parents	Child
	Attainment tests (e.g. reading, maths, language, spelling)	↕	↕		
1, 2	Criterion-referenced, curriculum-based assessments; placement tests	↕	↕		
3, 4, 5, 6, 7	Performance checklist; profiling; observation; record of achievement	↕	↕	'Child at Home' profile	Self-report
	Attitude inventories	↕	IQ and ability testing		

References key:
1. Akerman et al., 1983 (DATAPAC) 2. Ainscow and Tweddle, 1984 3. Pearson and Lindsay, 1986 4. Wolfendale, 1988 (and see Appendix 2) 5. Wolfendale and Bryans, 1989 (Learning Descriptive Observation Sheet in Appendix) 6. Ollendick and Hersen, 1984 7. Self-report (for examples see Appendix 3)

Table 3.2 *Intervention: options for key people*

References key

1, 2, 3, 4	*Devise individual programmes,* examples: Direct Instruction; precision teaching DATAPAC; parental involvement in reading Peer tutoring	*Classroom organisation* Room management (Chapter 5) Seating arrangements Groupwork Timetable
5, 6, 7, 8, 9	Children's self-monitoring and recording	
	Work with teachers and others Peripatetic/visiting advisory teacher School-based advisory/special needs co-ordinator Welfare assistants	*Work with support agencies* Educational psychologists Advisers Community languages Parents

References key:
1. SRA (1985)
2. Raybould and Solity (1985)
3. Akerman *et al.* (1983)
4. Topping and Wolfendale (1985)
5. Sprick (1981) – this is a comprehensive handbook covering nine topic areas in planning for learning and behaviour management
6. Lovitt (1984)
7. Wood (1984)
8. Willey (1985)
9. Topping (1988)

means of evaluation, are explored further in Chapters 5 and 7 respectively, in part because the subject matter of this chapter and that of Chapter 4 lend themselves to some common specifications for record-keeping and evaluation.

COLLECTIVE RESPONSIBILITY FOR MANAGING THE CURRICULUM

The planning and management of the curriculum rightly belongs primarily to curriculum and subject specialists. Where 'collective action' comes in is at points when teachers want to plan appropriate learning opportunities for individual children. The quotation from White and Haring (see earlier, p. 45) illuminates how each child's learning needs can be identified and planned for. As she or he moves through curriculum stages progress as well as 'sticking points' are likewise identified.

The formula, child/curriculum match is now applicable to the whole curriculum and not just in traditional approaches to 'failing' children, to the 'key' subjects of reading, mathematics. It is commonplace nowadays to come across arrangements that are an integral part of classroom practice where special needs/learning resource teachers are helping class teacher colleagues to plan and manage learning in general, and in particular, on behalf of children with special educational needs.

At the risk of labouring the theme, the point is that, whereas, once, opting out of mainstream curriculum into tangential remedial activities appeared to be a viable solution, the view now prevails that those 'failing' children's interests are not best served by distancing them from the mainstream. The same applies to children who have been or are in special school who are entitled to access to a broader spectrum of curriculum opportunity. Their protection, within the hurly-burly of an 'ordinary' school, comes from a carefully prepared 'statement of needs' – in this chapter's context a learning profile.

Within a framework of agreed and shared responsibility, there is a receptive climate to express and list at an early stage concerns felt about a child and not to wait until the problem becomes 'referrable'. 'Need' is relative; therefore, with the handicapping labels officially dropped, there is all the more reason to abolish the absolutes. The term 'remedial' should henceforth be eliminated from the educational lexicon.

Only if schools can move towards the notion of collective responsibility and corporate management to embrace 'special needs' can we avoid falling into the trap where the old-style remedial department becomes the new-titled special needs department, but separatist practice endures (Galloway, 1985) – a change of name will merely mean the same thing!

The curriculum audit and whole curriculum development plan called for by the National Curriculum Council (NCC, 1990) should foster a climate for encouraging collective responsibility but, too, facilitate special needs being incorporated as of right.

POSITIVELY PROMOTING LEARNING IN THE CONTEXT OF THE NATIONAL CURRICULUM

A spate of documents emphasises that the whole curriculum is more than the National Curriculum, though the proportion of time devoted to those subjects or activities that are neither core nor foundation subjects is lamentably low. The notion of entitlement is therefore to *all* curriculum opportunities for *all* pupils and this is a far broader conception than the parallel and limited remedial input ever was.

For special schools taking the National Curriculum on board it is proving to be a liberation and an enrichment to the conception of educating children with moderate and severe learning difficulties (Fagg *et al.*, 1990). Whilst writers are justifiably cautious, even reserved in their judgement as to whether or not 'working towards Level I' is a tenable concept (Daniels and Ware, 1990), nevertheless the message unmistakably reaching the ears of all in education is that special needs must not be marginalised.

Now, with a phalanx of professionals supporting class teachers (support, advisory teachers, welfare assistants, educational psychologists) it is entirely feasible that, for as long as earmarked funds are channelled to special needs (via LMS and formula funding, with central LEA money for 'statemented' pupils), each pupil in a primary school with possible or identified special needs can have a learning programme that:

- identifies current levels of attainment in appropriate core and foundation subjects (on the National Curriculum, baseline assessment, classroom-based observation and assessment, Learning Profile, Learner characteristics, see Norwich, 1990)
- takes account of and incorporates the cross-curricular themes (Aherne *et al.*, 1990; NCC, 1990)
- includes short-term learning targets as well as longer-term goals (Hampshire LEA, 1989b; SNIPP, 1990)
- has been task-analysed and broken down into learning sequences which are realistic within time-frames available (SNIPP, 1990)
- encourages learning according to an assessable hierarchy right across curriculum areas (Haring and Eaton, 1978)
- whilst being within the sequential approach of the National Curriculum, can be differentiated/modified flexibly according to his/her pace and style of learning as well as reflective of his/her interests and skill-acquisition need (*Portage in the Classroom*, 1987; Hampshire LEA, 1989b; Lewis, 1991)
- relates individual learning needs to the social learning contexts of the classroom and school
- is amenable to a range of types of assessment: SATs, if need be, National Curriculum Attainment Summaries (see Hampshire LEA, 1989a, 1990), teacher assessment, Records of Achievement, parental and pupil assessment (see Webster and Webster, 1990; Merttens and Vass, 1990; SEAC Packs)
- has access to technology, including information technology, as and when appropriate (Bowker, 1989; Goler, 1990; Montgomery, 1990).

The references cited (also NCC, 1989) comprise practical guidelines, books and packages designed to assist teachers, and their colleagues deliver the National Curriculum to children with a range of special needs.

The following list consists of a number of basic requisites to ensure access to all curriculum opportunities from a child-centred standpoint. The exhortation is tempered by acknowledgement not only of constraints everyone is subject to of time and resources, but also of the fact that some of the key concepts are ones that are the least researched, the ones with which many practitioners to date have had the least experience, in the area of mainstream primary school special needs, namely:

- differentiation: what is the fine line between individualising the curriculum and creating a separatist curriculum (McNicholas, 1989; Montgomery, 1990)?
- progression: this calls for unprecedented inter-teacher planning and co-operation (Montgomery, 1990)
- breadth, balance, relevance of curriculum experience: the lack hitherto of overall responsibility for special needs which perpetuated a fragmented, skills-driven remedial orientation gives way to a conception of curriculum which encompasses all statutory and non-statutory areas (McNicholas, 1989)
- modification: again, it is a fine line that divides a flexible, individualised adaptation of the National Curriculum subjects from one that marginalises a pupil from the rest of the class. What modification means in practice is developing expertise and experience in these activities: provision of alternative or extended topics, delaying start times to a topic or theme, devising a 'preliminary' programme, halting a programme, omitting topics and so on.

Many LEAs are devising local guidelines, building up 'case histories' of pupils on a modified curriculum, some of whom will have a statement of special educational needs, with explicit recommendations for curriculum modification.

To date, the National Curriculum Council has concerned itself more with content and processes of delivery of the Curriculum than it has deliberated on teaching style (though a study by NCC is currently under way). Here is a list of ideal teaching approaches and attributes. They call for a non-existent paragon to exhibit them consistently all of the time, but at least they can be on the agenda of planning for special needs, in schools and on in-service and on teaching training:

- creating meaningful relevant learning opportunities within the school
- choosing the appropriate 'teaching moment' to be pedagogical

- praising appropriately
- celebrating individual and group learning success
- providing the appropriate language of instruction for the task or request in hand
- encouraging co-operative learning
- offering a supportive, non-judgemental persona to each and every pupil.

None of the developments of recent years and in particular the arrival of the National Curriculum makes the radical formulation of Bloom (1983a, 1983b) less relevant or less timely. It stands the test of time, which is a rather sad commentary on the fact that teaching remains a conservative profession, rooted in conventional concepts of pedagogy, i.e. teaching means communicating facts and measuring outcomes. The challenge for educators is to assess the extent to which Bloom's five 'alterable variables' (briefly described below) can be applied within education and whether or not the 'new' climate engendered by the 1988 Education Reform Act encourages or inhibits his greatly broadened view of the teaching and learning processes.

BLOOM'S 'ALTERABLE VARIABLES'

Bloom's basic premise is that, as a result of recent educational research, we have a better understanding of teaching–learning factors. As a result, he feels, pupil learning can now be improved greatly, and it is possible to describe the favourable learning conditions that can enable virtually all pupils 'to learn to a high standard'.

1. *Available time versus time-on-task.* Bloom says that we ought to pay more attention to time spent as 'active learning time' rather than on considerations of what time is made available for learning, for not all pupils are equally 'on-task' at any one time. Studies show that the percentage of engaged (on-task) time is highly related to subsequent measures of achievement and to subsequent indices of interests and attitudes towards learning.

2. *Intelligence versus cognitive entry.* Bloom expresses the view that cognitive entry characteristics are more relevant to present and future learning than IQ measures as predictors of learning ability. These are the specific knowledge, abilities and skills that are the essential pre-requisites for learning a particular subject or task. They have a high relation with achievement and have an obvious causal effect on later achievement.

3. *Summative versus formative testing.* As with Gagné (1985), Bloom's work has been concerned with requisites and conditions for children achieving mastery at every level and stage; thorough mastery is an essential precursor for subsequent stages. Yet we have failed to develop and apply checking (formative) tests and procedures to verify each child's mastery level. Our summative tests (end of a course, end of term/year, examinations) are blunt, insensitive measures of progress as well as of task difficulty.

4. *Teachers versus teaching.* Bloom is critical of teachers' traditional practice, which is characterised by a method of proceeding that does not bring out the best in children, as some teachers unwittingly pay more attention to and therefore reward the faster learner.

5. *Parent status versus home environment processes.* In this 'alterable variable', Bloom juxtaposes specific curricular focus on mastery learning with broader, ecological considerations as to what parents and other adults significant in children's lives can contribute. On the basis of evidence, he says that it is clear that when home and school have 'congruent learning emphases' and shared aspirations (see Chapter 2, this book) the child has little difficulty in later school learning.

Bloom's optimistic views as to how schools might be enabled to alter expectations, attitudes, organisation and conditions for learning have been given prominence here because they are compatible with the themes and philosophies of this book and especially relevant to this chapter on learning.

It is not for want of trying that we have not found 'the holy grail' – the formulae by which children's (and adults') potential can be optimised. There is an honourable tradition of American psychologists who have worked for years hypothesis-testing into conditions for learning, e.g. Ausubel (1978), Gagné (1985), Bloom himself, others mentioned earlier and associated with the genesis of behavioural approaches.

Researchers and researcher-practitioners in America and the United Kingdom have focused on specific strategies to promote efficient learning, e.g. memory (Kail, 1984), learning style (Stott, 1978), and learning strategies (Nisbet and Shucksmith, 1986), learning how to learn (Novak and Gowin, 1984). They have provided teachers with a range of learning theories and their relevance to actual teaching (Bigge, 1982; Fontana, 1984a; Glynn, 1983; Riding, 1983; Stones, 1979); have presented the relationship between psychology and teaching (Francis, 1985; Entwhistle, 1987); and have formulated learning 'rules' to foster efficient learning (McIntire, 1984).

But we may still be evolving towards a synthesis between the identified requisites and conditions for learning and the applications
of theories of 'learning difficulties', which cannot finally be conceptualised differently from learning *per se*. If researchers could
empirically find common premises on which to investigate teaching/
learning difficulties we might yet find pragmatic solutions to many a
problem that has bedevilled teachers and especially how to reach each
child's teachable self and develop it to the hilt.

A FINAL WORD ABOUT THE LEARNER

Recently there have been concerted attempts to involve the learner
directly. In the main, behavioural approaches have paved the way for
use in mainstream and special school settings for a range of self-report,
self-monitoring materials, whilst the pupil profiling element within
Records of Achievement (that is, pupil self-assessment) has become
accepted and established in many LEAs. These and other methods of
directly involving the pupil in his/her own learning are listed and
described in Wolfendale (1990) including reference to co-operative
learning and peer tutoring (see, too, Appendix 3 of this book). In
general, then, there is a move towards self-directed learning at primary
and secondary levels (and see Montgomery, 1990) and in the
Wolfendale (1990) paper teachers are urged to promote 'PUPIL', an
acronym which stands for Promoting Universal Pupil Involvement in
Learning'!

Traditionally, children have not been encouraged to articulate their
views about themselves as learners – how they see their learning
assets; what are the obstacles to their learning; what best motivates
them; what activities they prefer; what keeps them on or off tasks; how
relevant they perceive to be the various classroom and activities in
which they engage.

The principle ought to be established, agreed, acted upon and
solutions found to bring children fully into the collaborative processes of meeting their needs. As Nisbet and Shucksmith (1986) point
out, learning in the future is likely 'to be characterised by a higher
degree of independent, self-motivated learning' and we need to
develop strategies 'which involve a higher level of self-monitoring
than teachers have been accustomed to expect from their pupils'
(pp. 91, 92).

REFERENCES

Aherne, P., Thorner, A. with Fagg, S. and Skelton, S. (1990) *Mathematics for All; An Interactive Approach with Level I*. Manchester: University of Manchester, School of Education.

Ainscow, M. and Muncey, J. (1983) Learning difficulties in the primary school, an inservice training initiative. *Remedial Education* 18 (3), 116–24.

Ainscow, M. and Muncey, J. (1984) *SNAP*. Cardiff: Drake Educational Associates.

*Ainscow, M. and Tweddle, D. (1979) *Preventing Classroom Failure: An Objectives Approach*. Chichester: Wiley.

Ainscow, M. and Tweddle, D. (1984) *Early Learning Skills Analysis*. Chichester: Wiley.

*Akerman, T., Gunelt, D., Kenward, P., Leadbetter, P., Mason, L., Matthews, C. and Winteringham, D.(1983) 'DATAPAC: an interim report'. Birmingham University: Department of Educational Psychology.

Ausubel, D. (1978) *Educational Psychology: A Cognitive View*, 2nd edn. London: Holt, Rinehart & Winston.

Becker, W., Engelmann, S., Carnine, D. and Rhine, W. (1981) 'Direct instruction model'. In Rhine, W. (ed.) *Making Schools More Effective, New Directions from Follow-Through*. New York: Academic Press.

Bigge, M. (1982) *Learning Theories for Teachers*, 4th edn. London: Harper & Row.

Bishop, M., Copley, M. and Porter, J. (eds) (1986) *Portage: More than a Teaching Programme*. Windsor: NFER-Nelson.

Bloom, B. (1983a) *All Our Children Learning*. New York: McGraw-Hill.

Bloom, B. (1983b) *Human Characteristics and School Learning*. New York: McGraw-Hill.

Bowker, P. (1989) Individualising the approach with the aid of IT. *Support for Learning* 4 (3) (August), 160–5.

Brennan, W. (1982) *Changing Special Education*. Milton Keynes: Open University Press.

Bullock, A. (Chair) (1975) *A Language for Life*. London: HMSO.

Cameron, R.J. (ed.) (1981) Curriculum objectives issue. *Remedial Education* 16 (4) (November).

*Croll, P. and Moses, D. (1985) *One in Five: The Assessment and Incidence of Special Educational Needs*. London: Routledge & Kegan Paul.

Daniels, H. and Ware, J. (eds) (1990) *Special Educational Needs and the National Curriculum*, Bedford Way series. London: Kogan Page/University of London.

Entwhistle, N. (1987) *Understanding Classroom Learning*. London: Hodder & Stoughton.

Fagg, S., Aherne, P., Skelton, S. and Thornber, A. (1990) *Entitlement for All in Practice: A Broad, Balanced and Relevant Curriculum for Pupils with Severe and Complex Learning Difficulties in the 1990s*. Manchester: University of Manchester, School of Education.

Farnham-Diggory, S. (1978) *Learning Disabilities*. London: Fontana/Open Books.

Fish, J. (1985) *Special Education: The Way Ahead*. Milton Keynes: Open University Press.

Fontana, D. (ed.) (1984a) *The Education of the Young Child*, 2nd edn. Oxford: Blackwell.

Fontana, D. (ed.) (1984b) *Behaviourism and Learning Theory in Education*. Edinburgh: Scottish Academic Press/BJEP.

Francis, H. (ed.) (1985) *Learning to Teach: Psychology and Teacher Training*. Lewes: Falmer Press.

Gagné, R. (1985) *The Conditions of Learning and Theory of Instruction*, 4th edn. London: Holt, Rinehart & Winston.

Gains, C. and McNicholas, J. (ed.) (1979) *Remedial Education: Guidelines for the Future*. Harlow: Longman.

Galloway, D. (1985) *Schools, Pupils and Special Educational Needs*. Beckenham: Croom Helm.

Glynn, T. (1983) 'Building an effective teaching environment'. In Wheldall and Riding, op. cit.

Goler, B. (1990) Computer use with children with special educational needs in primary schools. *British Journal of Special Education* 17 (2) (June), 66–9.

Gredler, G. (1989) 'Approaches to the remediation of learning difficulties: a current assessment'. In Gupta, R. and Coxhead, P. (eds) *Intervention with Children*. London: Routledge.

Gulliford, R. (1985) *Teaching Children with Learning Difficulties*. Windsor: NFER-Nelson.

Hampshire LEA (1989a) *National Curriculum Attainment Summaries Resources Pack*.

Hampshire LEA (1989b) *Meeting Special Educational Needs within the National Curriculum*.

Hampshire LEA (1990) *Recording Achievement Resource Pack*.

Haring, N. G. and Eaton, M. D. (1978) 'Systematic instructional procedures: an instructional hierarchy'. In Haring, N. G. *et al.* (eds) *The Fourth R – Research in the Classroom*. Columbus, OH: Charles E. Merrill.

Hirst, P. and Peters, R. S. (1970) *The Logic of Education*. London: Routledge & Kegan Paul.

Jewell, T. and Feiler, A. (1985) A review of behaviourist teaching approaches in the UK. *Early Child Development and Care* 20, 67–86.

Kail, R. (1984) *The Development of Memory in Children*, 2nd edn. New York: W. H. Freeman.

Kiernan, C. (1981) *Analysis of Programmes for Teaching*. Basingstoke: Globe Education.

Lewis, A. (1991) *The National Curriculum and Children with Difficulties in Learning*. London: Routledge.

Lister, T. and Cameron, R. J. (1986) Curriculum management: planning curriculum objectives. *Educational Psychology in Practice* 2 (1) (April).

Lovitt, T. (1984) *Tactics for Teaching*. Columbus, OH: Charles E. Merrill.

McBrien, J. (1981) Introducing the EDY project. *Special Education, Forward Trends* 8 (2), 29–36.

McCreesh, J. and Maher, A. (1974) *Remedial Education: Objectives and Techniques*. London: Ward Lock Educational.

McIntire, R. (1984) 'How children learn'. In Fontana (1984a), op. cit.

McNicholas, J. (1989) Curriculum implications of ERA. *Support for Learning* 4 (3), (August) 130–6.

Merttens, R. and Vass, J. (1990) *How to Plan and Assess the National Curriculum.* Oxford: Heinemann Educational.

Montgomery, D. (1990) *Children with Learning Difficulties.* London: Cassell.

NCC (1989) *Guidance No. 2: A Curriculum for All: Special Educational Needs in the National Curriculum.* York: National Curriculum Council.

NCC (1990) *Guidance No. 3: The Whole Curriculum.* York: National Curriculum Council.

Nisbet, J. and Shucksmith, J. (1986) *Learning Strategies.* London: Routledge & Kegan Paul.

Norwich, B. (1990) *Reappraising Special Needs Education.* London: Cassell.

Novak, J. and Gowin, D. (1984) *Learning How to Learn.* Cambridge: Cambridge University Press.

*Ollendick, T. and Hersen, M. (1984) *Child Behavioural Assessment: Principles and Procedures.* Oxford: Pergamon.

*Pearson, L. and Lindsay, G. (1986) *Special Needs in Primary Schools, Identification and Intervention.* Windsor: NFER-Nelson.

Portage in the Classroom (1987) Windsor: NFER-Nelson.

Potts, P. (1983) 'Summary and prospect'. In Booth, T. and Potts, P. (eds) *Integrating Special Education.* Oxford: Basil Blackwell.

Raybould, E. (1984) 'Precision teaching'. In Fontana (1984b), op. cit.

*Raybould, E. and Solity, J. (1985) 'Teaching with precision'. In Smith, op. cit.

Raymond, J. (1984) *Teaching the Child with Special Needs.* London: Ward Lock Educational.

Riding, R. (1983) 'Adapting instruction for the learner'. In Wheldall and Riding, op. cit.

SEAC (1989) *Teacher Assessment in the Classroom*, Pack A; *Teacher Assessment in the School*, Pack B; *A Course Book of Teacher Assessment*, Pack C School Examinations and Assessment Council, Newcombe House, 45 Notting Hill Gate, London W11 3JB.

Smith, C. (ed.) (1985) *New Directions in Remedial Education.* Lewes: Falmer Press.

SNIPP (Special Needs Individualised Programme Planning) (1990) Morpeth: Northumberland Education Department.

Solity, J. (1984) *An Introduction to Direct Instruction.* Warwick: University of Warwick.

Solity, J. and Bull, S. (1987) *Special Needs: Bridging the Curriculum Gap.* Milton Keynes: Open University Press.

*Sprick, R. (1981) *The Solution Book.* Henley-on-Thames: Science Research Associates.

*SRA (1985) *Direct Instruction: A Review.* Henley-on-Thames: Science Research Associates.

Stones, E. (1979) *Psychopedagogy: Psychological Theory and the Practice of Teaching.* London: Methuen.

Stott, D. (1978) *Helping Children with Learning Difficulties: A Diagnostic Teaching Approach.* London: Ward Lock Educational.

Strivens, J. (1981) 'Use of behaviour modification in special education: a critique'. In Barton, L. and Tomlinson, S. (eds) *Special Education: Policy, Practice and Social Issues*. London: Harper & Row.

Swann, W. (1985) 'Psychological science and the practice of special education'. In Claxton, G. *et al.*, *Psychology and Schooling: What's the Matter?* Bedford Way Papers No. 25. London: University of London, Institute of Education.

Tansley, A. and Gulliford, R. (1960) *The Education of Slow-learning Children*. London: Routledge & Kegan Paul.

Tansley, P. and Pankhurst, J. (1981) *Children with Specific Learning Difficulties*. Windsor: NFER-Nelson.

Thomas, G. (1985) What psychology had to offer education – then. *Bulletin BPS* **38**, 322–6.

Topping, K. (1988) *The Peer Tutoring Handbook*. London: Croom Helm.

*Topping, K. and Wolfendale, S. (eds) (1985) *Parental Involvement in Children's Reading*. Beckenham: Croom Helm.

Tweddle, D. and Pearson, L. (1984) 'The formulation and use of behavioural objectives'. In Fontana (1984b), op. cit.

Webster, A. and Webster, V. (1990) *Profiles of Development: Recording Children's Development within the National Curriculum*. AVEC Designs Ltd, PO Box 709, Bristol BS99 1GE.

Wedell, K. (1983) Assessing special educational needs. *NUT Secondary Education Journal* **13** (2) (June).

Welton, J., Wedell, K. and Vorhaus, G. (1982) *Meeting Special Educational Needs: The 1981 Education Act and Its Implications*, Bedford Way Papers No. 12. Tadworth: Heinemann Educational Books/University of London, Institute of Education.

Wheldall, K. (ed.) (1981) The behaviourist in the classroom: aspects of applied behavioural analysis in British educational contexts. *Educational Review*, Offset Publications No. 1. Birmingham: University of Birmingham, Department of Educational Psychology.

Wheldall, K. and Glynn, T. (1989) *Effective Classroom Learning*. Oxford: Basil Blackwell.

Wheldall, K. and Riding, R. (eds) (1983) *Psychological Aspects of Learning and Teaching*. Beckenham: Croom Helm.

White, D.R. and Haring, N.G. (1980) *Expectional Teaching*. Columbus, OH: Charles E. Merrill.

*Willey, M. (1985) *A Strategy for Early Intervention in Special Needs in the Ordinary School*, Perspectives no. 15 (March). Exeter: University of Exeter, School of Education.

Wolfendale, S. (1988) *The Parental Contribution to Assessment*. Developing Horizons, no. 10. Stratford-upon-Avon: National Council for Special Education.

Wolfendale, S. (1990) 'Collaboration between and with pupils'. Paper to 1989 Conference of the National Council for Special Education. NCSE, Exhall Grange, Wheelwright Lane, Coventry CV7 9HP.

Wolfendale, S. and Bryans, T. (1979) *Identification of Learning Difficulties: A Model for Intervention*. Stafford: National Association for Remedial Education.

*Wolfendale, S. and Bryans, T. (1980) Intervening with learning in the Infant School. *Remedial Education* 15 (1) (February).

Wolfendale, S. and Bryans, T. (1989) *Managing Behaviour*. Stafford: National Association for Remedial Education.

*Wood, J. (1984) *Adapting Instruction for the Mainstream*. Columbus, OH: Charles E. Merrill.

—4——

The management of behaviour in school

Distinguishing behaviour from learning by having two separate chapters is avowedly a somewhat artificial divide; yet one that is consistent with literature on the subjects. It is unfortunate that, for reasons to do with handling and processing vast amounts of information, we demarcate in this way, for it betokens a conceptual divide that does not exist in reality in or out of classrooms. Learning and motivation, self-esteem and behaviour in and out of class are inextricably bound up, as we all know. Even writers who make valiant attempts to present the interrelationship of learning and behaviour have to present separately techniques and programmes towards promoting learning, and changing and managing behaviour.

This chapter, then, has to abide by these distinctions for the purposes of discussing and presenting material within defined and delineated conceptual frameworks. However, the chapter follows on from Chapter 3 deliberately, so that the links and cross-matching are evident to and easily accomplished by the reader. The structure of this chapter also bears some similarity to that of the previous chapter.

There has been a proliferation, in recent years, of texts and manuals on dealing with 'troublesome and troubling' behaviour and a number of these will be referred to and invoked in this chapter. Such a surge in the literature reflects expressed concern over the perceived prevalence of disruptive behaviour and the growth of provision and development of 'technologies' and programmes to alter and manage behaviour. The same concern led to the setting up of the Committee of Enquiry chaired by Lord Elton to look into discipline in schools and make recommendations.

The preoccupation with 'difficult' behaviour is self-evidently due to the issues of control posed by any kind of deviant, antisocial behaviour. That is, teachers hope and expect to manage child behaviour in their classes and have expectations, as do parents, of individual behaviour and social interaction that conform to societal norms and prevailing moral codes. Lack of adherence to these norms interferes with lessons and class management in general and raises teachers' anxieties that they will not be able to teach, and that they may not have adequate strategies to avert, reduce, or change offending behaviour.

So, although in teacher training emphasis is given to setting classroom conditions to promote positive (conforming) behaviour, in reality the focus of attention and the spur of action is on preventing and coping with difficult and disturbing behaviour.

SCOPE OF THE CHAPTER

This book is about 'special' educational needs, that is to say, the distinct and identifiable 'needs' of children within schools, and how schools, in partnership with others, can devise and implement policies for ensuring that these are recognised and met. In Chapter 1 the principle of the basic rights of children to these considerations was introduced. The remit of Chapter 3 was to examine how children's learning needs could be provided for. This chapter examines how schools are organised to deal with behaviour and emotional difficulties. As importantly, it explores how schools can provide a learning and social environment that is conducive to children feeling settled, at ease, and motivated. We would all hope that children feel comfortable in school, are motivated to learn, enjoy a positive dialogue with teachers and peers, and for those under stress from other sources, find it a solace to be in school.

A prime aim of this chapter is to interrelate two major themes:

1. To present examples of recent and current work on identifying, assessing, and intervening with behaviour and emotional difficulties in primary schools.
2. To then examine how climates for positive behaviour can most effectively be created and maintained.

Towards achieving these aims, we will look at terminology and definitions, and briefly refer to concepts of aetiology and psychopathology within the context of the growth in provision for behaviour/emotional difficulties and disruptive behaviour. At the end of the chapter there will be an attempt to outline a policy on behaviour management that primary schools could adopt, within what could be termed a 'code of practice'.

The findings and impact of the Elton Report, which has been the biggest single marker in this area of 'discipline' for years, will be referred to, since they have repercussions on attitudes, provision and practice.

ISSUES OF TERMINOLOGY AND DEFINITION

Certain terms in education have become common currency, despite expressed reservations over their continued use. The Warnock Committee examined the concept of maladjustment and professed itself to be unhappy over the label with its confused, uncertain aetiology and consequent value-laden attributes. Maladjustment is, within the parameters of the Education Act 1981, a 'grey' area, as is the issue within LEAs as to whether or not 'maladjusted', 'disturbed', 'disruptive' children should be statemented. The decisions tend to depend on existing criteria within LEAs for admission to local provision (on- and off-site units, centres, schools, even home tuition).

The confusion over terminology is not surprising, since it mirrors the never-to-be-resolved debates about aetiology and cause and effect.

The literature reflects the search for ways to pin down, in epidemiological contexts, the elusive nature of the origins and incidence of behaviour and emotional problems. It also seeks to track down signs and symptoms of what might well be within the parameters of 'normal' social and emotional development (Rutter, Tizard and Whitmore, 1970; Shepherd, Oppenheim and Mitchell, 1971; Stott, Marston and Neill, 1975). The Warnock Report used these and other statistics, in part, to arrive at its percentage of children estimated to have special needs at any one time.

The main official category (up to the Education Act 1981) *maladjustment* has continued to vex educationalists and clinicians. Since Laslett's book (1977), which represented a theory–practice mix, there have been other books and chapters that give an examination and critique of the concept (Bowman, 1981; Stott, 1982), and Woolfe (1981) scrutinises the use of the term within the context of local authority decision making.

In order to make the label 'maladjustment' meaningful, there have been attempts to define it by listing behaviours that singly, or in combinations, have been said to be maladjusted (e.g. Underwood Report, 1955). Later, broadening the term to encompass disturbed/disturbing behaviour, and to include signs of psychiatric relevance, Rutter proposed 11 categories (1965) and Stott, Marston and Neill proposed some based on their own research (1975). Later still, Rutter (1975) put forward nine main criteria by which to gauge the extent of a child's behavioural or emotional disturbance. For the practitioner, these can be useful indices but they cannot be regarded as fixed or invariable, whether the signs and symptoms come as 'single spies' or in 'battalions'.

The psychopathological literature is vast and sources used in Great Britain are mainly, but not wholly, American. They relate survey, epidemiological and clinical data back to aetiological behavioural and sociological data, and thence to data from treatment and its results. Recommended texts are Achenbach (1982), Morris and Kratochwill (1983), Rhodes and Paul (1978), Schwartz and Johnson (1981). They and other such tomes represent valiant attempts to pin down elusive human behaviour, its conforming as well as deviant characteristics. Naturally, terms, concepts, explanations and data from one set of theoretical constructs may not be compatible with those of another, thus the semantic confusion alluded to above is perpetuated by the existence of a number of competing frameworks, each, moreover, with differing historical origins.

Other labels have been adopted as working terms, such as 'disturbed', 'disturbing', 'troubled', 'troublesome', 'deviant', 'delinquent', 'antisocial'. The demarcation between 'neurotic' and 'conduct' disorders (Rutter, 1965) can be seen to be an attempt to neaten the semantic untidiness.

Another factor to take into account is the changing fashion in deeming aspects of behaviour to be a problem. Williams (1977) noted that teachers in the 1920s expressed concerns about children's sexual behaviour whereas nowadays they are more concerned about disruptive antisocial or aggressive behaviour. Folklore decrees that, at any one period in history, child and adolescent behaviour is alleged to be worse than at any other. The 'moral panic' (Cohen, 1972) of contemporary times is reflected and, of course, nurtured by strident media headlines announcing that the latest survey shows the behaviour of schoolchildren from infant school age upwards to be worse and more out of control than ever. Social conformity hits no headlines! Indeed the Elton Committee was set up partly in response to the 'moral panic' climate fostered and nurtured by the media.

A final comment on the fickleness of concepts and labels to do with children's behaviour that causes concern and generates emotions: children's behaviour is invariably reported by adults and it is adults who define 'problem' behaviour. Often such judgements may be little more than reflections of arbitrary and subjective biases on the part of adults, or else of their limits of tolerance (Wolfendale and Bryans, 1979).

ISSUES OF SOCIAL CONTROL

As long as societies and communities retain notions of acceptable/ unacceptable behaviour, and devise a range of sanctions to contain, control and punish, then likewise schools and educators cannot realistically expect to find simplistic solutions to endemic and core societal and human issues. This is especially so whilst, in global terms, strife and wars are as much part of the human condition as ever they have been.

This is a preamble to acknowledging that, irrespective of the terminology we employ, and stripped of clinical and therapeutic explanations, we retain, as a bottom line, the notion of control. Any kind of maladaptive behaviour is deviant and a departure from the inhouse rules, and social and moral codes (Hargreaves, Hester and Mellor, 1975). Teachers take very properly and seriously their ability or inability to control (to contain or redirect) the behaviour of individuals or groups.

It is arguable whether or not educational provision for disruptive children is benignly therapeutic or benignly controlling. Teachers may be viewed as 'friendly policemen/women' in another guise, no less agents of social control than are 'real' policemen and policewomen, and schools may be seen as actually producing disaffection (Booth and Coulby, 1987).

Ford, Mongon and Whelan (1982) express profound unease with the whole referral, assessment, labelling and placement processes. They assert that even setting up such processes predisposes us to look for and find stereotypes to fit the bill, i.e. fill the provision, whether it is a local off-site unit for disruptives or a residential school for maladjusted children. They contend that special educational provision cannot simply be accepted as a demonstration of philanthropic concern for the pupils but that the use of labelling in conjunction with special education is potentially an oppressive force. They perceive that professionals who play their part in these processes are collusive and perpetuate these inherent forces.

Denis Mongon is also one of the authors of a book in this series (Mongon *et al.*, 1989) in which these themes are elaborated. To that extent, this chapter is a trailer to an in-depth scrutiny of labelling, attitudes and provision, and aims to dovetail into that book. The issues raised in this chapter, and the measures proposed to combat and solve identified problems, are to be viewed as part of a primary school's overall responses and strategies towards special needs.

Whilst issues of social control may be at the heart of the matter, nevertheless, the collective responsibility which is the central message of this book must be predicated upon the relativities of deviant behaviour. Simplistic sets of sanctions, invoking rules, threatening disciplinary measures, have been shown merely to contain but never to solve any one school's problems of unrest and dissident behaviour. How schools can evolve coherent sets of strategies is pursued through the rest of the chapter. Alternative provision, as a backcloth and supplement to mainstream, is referred to later on.

PRIMARY SCHOOLS AS SOCIAL AND LEARNING
ENVIRONMENTS: TEACHERS' CONCERNS

The term 'behaviour' has been used loosely as a 'catch all'. It refers to
individual responses, interaction with the environment, social interaction in twos or in groups. It includes verbal as well as non-verbal
means of communication and the interpretation of people's behavioural repertoires by other people.

Children in class and in playgrounds are continually translating
social signals and cues and acting and responding accordingly – as are
adults. Within schools, the social system that works in a largely self-
regulatory way, with minor conflicts, demarcation disputes and mis-
understandings being fairly speedily resolved, breaks down when
teachers acknowledge that it is out of their direction and control and is
literally unmanageable. Mostly it is individuals who challenge and
upset the system, though teachers and psychologists are entirely
familiar with the associated phenomenon of a corresponding rise in the
social temperature of a given class.

There has been, during the last ten years, a spate of texts for teachers
that aim to assist them in identifying and expressing their concerns, and
thence to devising strategies for intervening. Leach and Raybould
(1977) went to great pains to shift attitudes away from within-child
and child-deficit models (see Chapter 1 of this book) to explain 'naughti-
ness' and nuisance behaviour, and likewise to reduce dependency on
the prejudice that children who are badly behaved in class tend to come
from 'poor', 'inadequate' homes with uncaring parents or with a sole
parent. They and other writers (Wolfendale and Bryans, 1989) have
encouraged the redefinition of problem behaviour into descriptors,
and have advanced techniques of identification and intervention that
exclude and bypass the pitfalls of ascribing cause to presumed effects.
Their suggested strategies include observing, describing, listing and
recording as precursors to action, whether it be individually focused
programmes (see below), group and class management (Robertson,
1989; Fontana, 1985), or emphasis on inservice and support within
schools (Hanko, 1985). Yet other writers have adopted a case study
format, thus providing exemplars – the principles from which practitioners can derive their own practice (Murgatroyd, 1980; Harrop,
1983; Morgan, 1984; Merrett, 1985).

Often these texts have been a response to teachers' oft-expressed
need to have more readily available strategies for recognising and
dealing with unwanted behaviour. Their concerns centre on their
justifiable goal of both teaching and managing efficiently, and
reconciling these goals with their responsibility to meet children's needs
in school.

The section that follows draws together a number of recent and current approaches, examining first those within behavioural frameworks since these are, to date, the most productive and consistently pragmatic.

RESPONDING TO BEHAVIOUR DIFFICULTIES

With reference to behavioural frameworks

Many of the volumes that comprise the behavioural 'stable' are manuals that present a rationale, followed by a step-by-step presentation of strategies and examples of record-keeping. Explicit in many of these is the acknowledgement that the trigger that inspires action is unwanted behaviour, though of course the longer-term goal is to create, maintain and manage positive behaviour.

Earlier pace-setters were Poteet (1973) and Ackerman (1972), both of whom introduced the idea of situational analysis, basing measurement on observation and recording and providing an ample number of techniques to modify behaviour, build in rewards, and maintain change.

Rationales. Behaviourists cut through what they see as 'fuzzy' unclear descriptions and explanations of maladaptive behaviour and prefer to concentrate on what can be done here and now to prevent a problem worsening and to ameliorate it. Cheesman and Watts (1985) set out a ten-point charter summarising their underlying assumptions. Central to its theme is that:

- behaviour is learned
- if it has not been learned it can be taught
- most child behaviour problems are simply excess or deficits of behaviour common to all children.
- learning must be within a social context
- the teacher is the most appropriate change agent within schools.

Herbert (1981), Morgan (1984), McGregor McMaster (1982), Wheldall, Merrett and Glynn (1986) and Bull and Solity (1987) stake out similar principles.

Features of behavioural approaches

All advocate stringently delineated sequences of action. For example, Lane (1986) outlines these phases: definition, assessment, formulation, intervention, follow-up. The BATPACK course (The Behavioural

Approach to Teaching Package: Wheldall and Merrett, 1984) consists of these units:

- identifying troublesome behaviour
- having an overview of the behavioural approach to teaching
- focusing on good behaviour; practising positives
- achieving the right classroom setting
- dealing with more troublesome behaviour
- tactics and implementation.

McGregor McMaster sets out five systematic stages: observations, definition, availability (determining the available reinforcers), deciding which to use, and action.

Behaviours to be changed

Succinctly, most behaviours are considered to be amenable to change. The literature is full of case study, single and group designs and their outcomes. Some of these have already been cited. Thus, no teacher or other child-carer need feel that intractable behaviour cannot be modified, no matter how severe the aggression, disruption, compulsive/obsessive acts, withdrawal, lack of co-operation, etc.

Teacher inservice training and support

A lot of the earlier behaviour modification was designed as individual, child-focused intervention, responding to need, to children 'referred' for one reason or another. Later, as the techniques became more refined and the results of single-case treatment convincing, the methodology was developed to such a point that training could be given to teachers. Current examples of seminal inservice approaches are BATPACK (reference above) for primary schools and PAD (Preventive Approaches to Disruption: Tweddle, 1986) for secondary schools. Features of inservice training packages are that the manuals are concise, sequential, case study illustrated, with back up video and take-away material which allows for discussion, role-play, and learning by doing.

These models of INSET have been taken up and adapted for LEA use. Training courses and materials for behaviour management in schools based on behavioural approaches have been developed in a number of LEAs and, as we shall see below, such initiatives have been given a boost since the publication of the Elton Report and inservice and development grants made available.

Limitations and critique of behavioural approaches

Proponents of behavioural approaches argue that the numerous case studies of successful application of principles into practice justify the rationale and the methods. They argue that, given the brief to improve, modify behaviour by changing the conditions (introducing rewards, applying consistent sanctions, involving children directly, where possible, as self-recorders), if success results, that is sufficient justification.

However, as we saw in Chapter 3, the criticism goes beyond purely pragmatic criteria to encompass moral, philosophical, social issues. Harrop (1983) in his final chapter faces up squarely to some of the issues. But even those who are uneasy about the concepts and methods, and are sympathetic to attitudes discussed earlier in the chapter about schools being agencies of social control, may acknowledge that behavioural approaches can be one coherent strategy within a rather more eclectic armoury of approaches to understanding and dealing with deviant and disaffected behaviour (Hughes, 1988; Davie, 1989).

With reference to other approaches

This section sub-divides, to look at within-school intervention, including referring to and co-working with support agencies, and concludes with reference to alternative provision.

Within-school

Traditionally there has been little sustained support and treatment directed at and taking place in schools, particularly primary schools. In part acknowledging this lack, one British study (Kolvin *et al.*, 1981) aimed to identify and characterise psychiatric and educational difficulties in children and to compare different ways of helping them overcome these difficulties. Four treatment approaches, over a period of up to a couple of years, were tested: behaviour modification, nurture work, parent–counselling teacher consultations, and group therapy. Studies were made of 265 children in junior schools and 309 in secondary schools.

The best junior results were in the group therapy regime and to a lesser extent in the nurture work programme, whilst in the secondary schools the 'best' approaches were the behaviour modification and group therapy. However, the 'small print' of this ambitious and complex study repays reading and is thought-provoking, not only about 'best treatment buys', but about the personnel support needed to sustain such programmes.

Counselling in schools has had a patchy, chequered history in Britain. It has been advocated with varying degrees of enthusiasm at different times and there are inservice courses for teachers. But there has never been the sort of take-up in British schools that has been seen in North America, where counsellors on high school staffs are common. It has never been seen as a priority in resource allocation and maybe, too, there has traditionally been an unwillingness to acknowledge that behaviour and emotional problems in schools are the proper province of teachers.

Sisterson (1983) makes a case for the development of pupil counselling in primary schools and advocates the incorporation of counselling training into teacher training. In the same journal, which is on the theme of guidance and counselling, there is an attempt to regenerate interest in counsellor education. One of the authors, Raymond, has since developed ideas (1985) as to what teachers can do in primary and secondary schools about presenting problems as well as positively fostering social and life skills. She is explicit about teachers' legitimate role in the area of pastoral care. Her work, as well as that of Thacker (1985), will be used as referents in this chapter when considering constructive approaches to promoting positive behaviour.

Schools and support agencies working in co-operation

The emphasis here is on within-school action taken largely by professionals. The involvement of parents on problem definition and intervention with behaviour and emotional difficulties will be considered later.

The recent growth of co-operative endeavours has in part arisen from dissatisfaction with traditional practice, which tended to polarise emotional/behavioural problems into referrable or non-referrable and what was and was not the province of schools or other agencies such as social services, psychological services, and child guidance.

Examples of recent work that demonstrates the effectiveness of co-operation between schools and services included the support team's work in some ILEA schools (Coulby and Harper, 1985), Hanko's teacher training and support work in schools (1985), the joint systems approach of Campion (1985) and Dowling and Osborne (1985). Coulby and Harper view the provision of the support team as part of school and LEA strategy to dealing with and preventing problems.

Conoley and Conoley (1982), drawing on their teaching, research and practice, put forward a model of school consultation, the core element of which is the relationship between the consultant (educational psychologist, social worker, counsellor, for example) and teachers. Consultants give on-the-job training in counselling skills, and advise and support teachers in setting up counselling and management programmes.

Beyond school: referral to other agencies

Warnock saw a key facet of the teacher's role as that of recognising and identifying children's learning and behaviour problems. There has already been some discussion regarding the criteria that determine the definition of a problem. Much inservice is directed to these very issues, e.g. SNAP (see Chapters 3 and 6).

Part of a teacher's skills in detecting emerging and existing problems is to recognise their severity. Many teachers say that they are not sufficiently knowledgeable about gauging severity and typology and correspondingly are uncertain as to which are appropriate referring agencies. In my previous post as an educational psychologist, we ran a course for teachers from primary and secondary schools entitled 'Criteria for Referral' that included speakers from local services describing their work. The participants perceived the value of the course as lying in the fact that they had discussed problem-recognition, how to keep situation records, when and to whom to refer. A referral grid was introduced that was subsequently adopted by some of the schools.

Teachers may or may not be kept informed as to treatment and therapy methods employed by other agencies. Family therapy has become increasingly popular and a variety of counselling approaches can be directed to one client, e.g., the child, or other members of the family (Egan, 1982; Nelson-Jones, 1988).

There are problem areas in which it is increasingly acknowledged that teachers play a key role. Child abuse and child sexual assault are examples of where a multidisciplinary approach is now seen to be vital (Porter, 1984; Parton, 1985; Maher, 1987). Inservice training and support are being offered to teachers to help them to spot signs of abuse and interference and associated stress (Elliott, 1985). Local authorities have developed inter- and across-agency procedures and codes of practice and, as part of this network, have introduced their own identification and action procedures in which teachers play an integral role (DES letter, July 1990).

The phenomenon of bullying is one that is receiving increasing attention and was examined by the Elton Committee. Particularly well researched in Scandinavia, bullying is now acknowledged to be a widespread activity that has persisted over centuries, is familiar to all of us, and is now seen to be the responsibility of teachers, governors, parents and pupils alike (Besag, 1989; Tattum and Lane, 1989).

The practical manuals of Tattum and Herbert (1990), Elliott/ KIDSCAPE (1990) and Elliott (1991) make it explicit that preventive and active responses are called for on the part of teachers. A DES-funded project based at Sheffield University aims to test out a whole-school policy on bullying involving 24 schools initially (Smith and Thompson, 1991).

Attention is also turning to the age-old activities of children in the playground, since playground behaviour is a mixture of positive social learning and interaction, and at the same time, for some, a source of stress, anxiety and isolation. The practical handbook by Ross and Ryan (1990) is applicable to teachers, welfare assistants, lunchtime supervisors, other professionals and parents (see also Imich and Jefferies, 1989).

Even, then, in the area of presenting problems, where once the demarcation between school and specialist services was clear-cut, we are beginning to see increased and better contact between the services as well as all the involved adults.

Alternative provision

Passing reference must be made to the provision that is made to those children who, by virtue of the severity of their disruptive behaviour, and/or emotional disturbance, are beyond being coped with in ordinary schools. Such provision is beyond the remit of this chapter but is a 'grey area' and needs mentioning.

The proliferation in recent years of on- and off-site units, schools and residential centres has been described and attempts have been made to evaluate their effectiveness (Galloway *et al.*, 1982; Topping, 1983; Mortimore *et al.*, 1983; Lloyd-Smith, 1984).

These chronicles paint a picture of confusing variability between LEAs as to criteria for admission, discharge and regime. Many LEAs have not addressed the issue as to whether or not children placed in units, but still on the roll of their mainstream schools, should have 'the protection of a statement'. It remains to be seen whether, within LMS, there will be moves to provide:

- more on-site units
- better service co-ordination
- skilled support staff
- more finance to provide other back-up resources
- systems of record-keeping
- stringent monitoring of children's progress and evaluation of the effectiveness of such provision.

SHARING CONCERNS: TOWARDS COLLECTIVE RESPONSIBILITY FOR MANAGING BEHAVIOUR

A picture having been sketched of trends in provision and methods of dealing with, in the main, unwanted behaviour, attention now turns to tangible strategies primary schools could adopt. The aim is to link these recent developments, which are not widespread, with the direct, practical steps schools can take to implement a policy of collective responsibility for special needs.

As with Chapter 3, it is not possible to provide exhaustive ideas within one chapter, so the emphasis will be upon key concepts which could act as a stimulus to further ideas. The parallels with Chapter 3 are intentional and one of its main messages is equally applicable to this chapter – namely, that the nub of school-based action is the relative contribution and input of several identified key people in relation to one or more children.

In the realm of behavioural and emotional difficulties, teamwork could operate over:

• sharing concerns
• agreeing and carrying out action
• overviewing the school's provision
• generally taking collective responsibility.

Broad representation would comprise core school and support staff, parent representation and the presence of others from supporting services.

Profiling

In Chapters 1 and 3 learning profiles were introduced and discussed, and a formula advanced for compiling one for each child. Consonant with the idea of a child profile that concentrates on maximising learning and dealing with learning difficulties, the same concept can be applied to behavioural aspects in general, and particularly to identified difficulties. Apter (1982) describes the formulation of a profile within an ecological framework and gives a case-study example of an ecological profile of a 'behaviourally disordered' pupil. There are striking similarities in terms of goal setting and sequences between this approach and that described in Chapter 3, which was 'home-grown' and predated Apter's publication.

Following on, then, from the exemplar in the previous chapter, the same format will be adopted, namely, singling out two major features of a child profile with reference to behavioural difficulties. These are assessment and intervention, and they are presented in Tables 4.1 and

Table 4.1 Assessing problem behaviour: options for key people

References key	Class teacher	Support/advisory teacher	Educational psychologists	Parents	Child
1, 2, 3, 4, 5, 6, 7, 8, 9	Behaviour checklists; rating scales; identifying; listing concerns		→		Self-report; self-record
10				'Child at Home' parental profile; observing and recording	
11, 12	Personality inventories; attitude scales		→		

References key:
1. Galvin and Singleton (1984) 2. Wolfendale and Bryans (1989) for the Personal Descriptive Observation sheet 3. Leach and Raybould (1977) 4. Coulby and Harper (1985) see Behaviour checklist (p. 69) 5. Apter (1982) 6. Achenbach (1985) 7. Ollendick and Hersen (1984) 8. Analysis of Coping Style (Boyd and Johnson, 1981) 9. Westmacott and Cameron (1981) 10. 'Parental profiling' (Wolfendale, 1988) and see Appendix 2 11. Bristol Social Adjustment Guides (Stott) 12. Self-reporting: see Appendix 3.

4.2 to illustrate the collective approach. As before, a key reference list is given of approaches, techniques, workable strategies. This listing is a compact way of bringing together a number of practical possibilities and is designed to save time in delving and cross checking. As with the references in Chapter 3, the references cited in the following section are asterisked in the reference list at the end of this chapter for readers wishing to design and carry out programmes.

Table 4.2 *Intervening with problem behaviour: options for key people (suggested framework)*

References key	Individual programmes	Group programmes	Classroom control and organisation
1, 2, 3, 4, 5, 6, 7, 8, 9	e.g. BATPACK SNAP	**10**, Social skills **11, 12** Life skills	**13** Robertson (1989) **14** TIPS (1985) **15** Nottingham University (1980) **16** Wood (1984) **17** Fontana (1985)
	Work with other teachers		*Work with support agencies and parents*
	18 Hanko (1985) **19** Coulby and Harper (1985) **20** Conoley and Conoley (1982) **21** Wolfendale (1988) **22** Harris (1983) **23** Westmacott and Cameron (1981) **24** Rogers (1991)		Educational Psychology Service Child Guidance Education Welfare Service Social Services

References key:
  1. BATPACK (Wheldall and Merrett, 1984)
  2. SNAP (Coventry Special Needs Action Programme: see Chapter 6)
  3. Raymond (1985)
  4. Cheesman and Watts (1985)
  5. Walker and Shea (1984)
  6. Herbert (1981)
  7. Harrop (1983)
  8. Sprick (1981)
  9. Lovitt (1984)
 10. Spence and Shepherd (1983)
 11. Thacker (1985)
 12. Hopson and Scally (1981)

PROMOTING POSITIVE BEHAVIOUR

1. Within the social climate of the school

The last section in this chapter is concerned with the broader social and ecological climate of schools, within which positive individual and group behaviour can flourish. A number of major focuses are brought together to form part of a school's overall strategy for fostering and maintaining positive relationships between peers and adults. Still within the context of teamwork, in principle it ought to be feasible for social situations, whether in classroom or playground, not to get out of hand if:

1. Personnel have identified tasks, and pre-agreed responses.
2. The response strategies are clearly seen as being part of the school's policy on behaviour management (see below).

Staff could engage in debate as to their aims for promoting positive behaviour out of which the following wishes might emerge:

- to promote social integration and ensure that children with special needs will be fully accepted in class and at play
- to provide for the development of social and life skills, either incidentally or by planned intervention

Each of these aims can be translated into medium- and longer-term objectives with corresponding programmes designed to achieve them. A few words to expand these aims follow.

Social integration.   The literature on this aspect is fairly voluminous. Hegarty, who has written the foundation book for this series, *Meeting Special Needs in the Ordinary School*, writes elsewhere (1982) of findings from integration studies that the personal and social benefits to all children are manifest and long-lasting. He summarises the perceived advantages in these words:

> The school can develop and grow richer as a social institution from having a wider range of social behaviours enacted in it and a broader spectrum of relationships available to its pupils and staff. There is a symbolic component as well; the presence of pupils with special needs in a school can imply important statements about the nature of the school, its tolerance for diversity and its regard for individuals. (p. 104)

The notion of friendships within school is one that has hitherto received scant attention with regard to teachers actually facilitating personal and social links. We may be back to issues of social manipulation posed at the outset of the chapter. However, an espoused policy on integration must include views on how to reverse social and public attitude to handicap and disability to ensure that children with special needs have an equal niche within the mainstream of social interaction. Rubin (1980) and Hartup (1978) provide overviews on children's friendships and Asher and Gottman (1981) bring together a number of perspectives on the evolution of friendships, including that between handicapped and non-handicapped children.

Play is a related area that would be worth exploring, for as Smith (1986) points out 'it would be helpful to know more about . . . whether certain forms of play provide particularly useful experience and opportunity for social skills and friendship formation' (p. 13).

Social and life skills.   These are areas that have burgeoned in recent years. Spence and Shepherd (1983) edited a volume that critically examined a number of programmes and their underlying rationales. These have been founded on twin tracks; firstly to make good perceived deficits in social skills, and secondly, to ensure that all children can benefit from such training.

The research still seems to be equivocal on the longer-term effectiveness. Notwithstanding what it can reveal, there have been recent moves to incorporate into or relate to the curriculum various approaches that come under the broad headings of social and life skills. Davies (1983) makes a valid distinction between these skills, though in reality it is probably difficult to demarcate clearly between social competence in handling life situations and competence in handling relationships.

Much of the work has taken place in secondary schools, but some of it has recently been tried out with younger children (Thacker, 1985). The work of Hopson and Scally (1981), for example, could serve as a model for adapting to primary schools, on the grounds that preparation for citizenship should start then.

2. Within the ecology of the school

Much of the preceding discussion has concentrated on the 'micro' of dealing with individual children's behaviour, though references to classroom organisations were included on the intervention chart (Table 4.2). As with learning difficulties and remediation, approaches to behaviour management have been tacked uneasily alongside the main curriculum.

A whole-school approach to learning and behaviour difficulties is increasingly seen as synonymous with meeting children's special needs. Apter's (1982) elaboration of the ecological concept fleshes out the practice of devising and implementing a through-school, within-community strategy. Cooper and Upton (1991) propose an eco-system approach to problem behaviour. Fontana (1985) urges teachers to appraise their own strategies within the context of their schools' organisation. Topping (1986) casts a critical eye over the organisation subsystems of schools that fail to build in safeguards for meeting children's needs and Pollard's title *The Social World of the Primary School* (1985) makes it explicit that schools serve a prime social function as well as being the place of learning. Pollard's thesis is that schools therefore have a responsibility to creating positive 'social worlds' for children, thus facilitating their learning.

The ecological perspective, then, embraces parental involvement. See Wolfendale (1990) for a model of a whole-school approach to behaviour management that includes parents as of right. Four levels are posited:

1. Current provision for dealing with behaviour problems.
2. The school system and current practice on involving parents.
3. School-focused INSET and identifying training needs for working with parents.
4. Direct work with parents and children.

How these four levels form a whole-school approach is explored in some detail.

A SCHOOL POLICY ON BEHAVIOUR MANAGEMENT: TOWARDS A CODE OF PRACTICE

To try to contain the complexity of this subject within the confines of one chapter is bound to appear glib; to attempt to define a policy for primary schools within the same chapter might merely sound presumptuous. However, the same logic that has guided the discussion to this point underscores the recommendation for school policy, that is, it is only by concerted and co-ordinated action that schools can solve their problems and seek to evolve strategies that realise their aims.

There may be a number of identifiable requisites to as well as constraints upon the promotion of a school policy that is publishable and available to pupils, parents, governors, the LEA. Several guiding principles are offered to stimulate debate. The most that may be realistic and attainable may be for a school to explicitly acknowledge that, whilst its *code of conduct* reflects society's expectations, the rules and sanctions of an individual school are unique to that school.

That being so, it is part of the accountability of the school to publish:

• clear expectations of adherence to its rules
• its system of sanctions for each breach of rules and regulations

Pupils and parents could expect to be informed as to the system of graded differential punishments that would reflect, proportionately, the severity of the offence (often sanctions are *ad hoc*, arbitrary, and conform to no agreed code). Any lack of observance of the agreed rules would not only invoke the appropriate sanction but, as importantly, would trigger into action the agreed procedure, to involve at once the pupil concerned and his or her parents. Restoration rather than dwelling on punishment would be the cardinal goal. By this means the pupil would be enabled to be directly involved within a positive framework of jointly attempting to solve the problem, agreeing a course of action, and, most fundamentally, meeting each child's unique need (Watkins and Wagner, 1987).

THE IMPACT AND EFFECTS OF THE ELTON REPORT

The climate of thinking surrounding the Elton Report was mentioned at the beginning of the chapter. There are divided views on the Report's impact. One view (unsubstantiated but often propagated informally and anecdotally) is the cynical line that a government-inspired report would and could not have much effect at the 'grassroots' level in classroom practice. Hand in hand with this stance is a view expressed by one or two of the teaching unions that the Elton Report did not sufficiently acknowledge the extent and seriousness of attacks upon teachers by pupils, nor the rising levels of violence within schools.

Diametrically opposed views consider that such a government report is:

(a) a useful lever and reference point and puts the whole issue firmly onto the educational agenda;

(b) a means of securing and generating central and local funds for provision of service training (cf. GRIST, then LEATGS, now GEST (Activity no. 13 for 1991), and the Education Support Grant (ESG category no. 33 for 1990–91).

(c) a starting point for appraisal of attitudes and school-based practice. In particular the Elton Report has spawned articles on whole-school policies for behaviour management and discipline, stemming from its own recommendations (Atkinson, 1989; Cooper and Upton, 1991);

(d) a stimulus for developing local and nationally available materials to support teacher inservice education, which the Report certainly has done (Northumberland LEA, 1989; Wiltshire LEA, 1989; Galvin, Mercer and Costa, 1990; Oxford Polytechnic, 1990)

(e) a means of promoting inter-professional working links (Wolfendale, Fox and Hayes, 1991) and pupil and parental involvement in setting and maintaining discipline and behaviour management policies;

(f) a confirmation of the link between underachievement and disaffected behaviour, from cited evidence;

(g) an affirmation of the principle of collective responsibility – from class teacher to corporate levels of the LEA, government and society.

Of course, one feasible view is that all of the above-listed positive features and findings of the Elton Report amount to continued forms of social control, albeit benign. But the daily reality of class teachers and their perennial problems of control and management are expressed succinctly by Elton:

> Our survey shows that teachers see talking out of turn and other forms of persistent, low-level disruption as the most frequent and wearing kinds of classroom misbehaviour. Low-level disruption is not a new feature of classroom life. (p. 67)

What the Elton Report contains by way of findings and recommendations is consistent with the information and messages contained in this chapter.

REFERENCES

Achenbach, T. (1982) *Development Psychopathology*, 2nd edn. Chichester: John Wiley.

*Achenbach, T. (1985) *Assessment and Taxonomy of Child and Adolescent Psychopathology*. Beverly Hills, CA: Sage Publications.

Ackerman, M. (1972) *Operant Conditioning Techniques for the Classroom Teacher*. Glenview, IL: Scott Foresman.

*Apter, S. (1982) *Troubled Children, Troubled Systems*. Oxford: Pergamon.

Asher, S. and Gottman, J. (eds) (1981) *The Development of Children's Friendships*. Cambridge: Cambridge University Press.

Atkinson, J. (1989) Responding to Elton: a whole-school approach. *Support for Learning* 4 (4) (November).

Besag, V. (1989) *Bullies and Victims in Schools*. Milton Keynes: Open University Press.

Booth, T. and Coulby, D. (eds) (1987) *Producing and Reducing Disaffection*. Milton Keynes: Open University Press.

Bowman, I. (1981) 'Maladjustment: a history of the category'. In Swann, W. (ed.) *The Practice of Special Education*. Oxford: Basil Blackwell.

*Boyd, H. and Johnson, G. (1981) *Analysis of Coping Style, A Cognitive-Behavioural Approach to Behaviour Management*. Westerville, OH: Charles E. Merrill.

Bull, S. and Solity, J. (1987) *Classroom Management: Principles to Practice*. Beckenham: Croom Helm.

Campion, J. (1985) *The Child in Context: Family-Systems Theory in Educational Psychology*. London: Methuen.

*Cheesman, P. and Watts, D. (1985) *Positive Behaviour Management, A Manual for Teachers*. Beckenham: Croom Helm.

Cohen, S. (1972) *Folk Devils and Moral Panics*. St Albans: McGibbon & Kee.

*Conoley, J. and Conoley, C. (1982) *School Consultation: A Guide to Practice and Training*. Oxford: Pergamon.

Cooper, P. and Upton, G. (1991) Controlling the urge to control: an ecosystemic approach to problem behaviour in schools. *Support for Learning 6* (1) (February).

*Coulby, D. and Harper, T. (1985) *Preventing Classroom Disruption*. Beckenham: Croom Helm.

Davie, R. (1989) 'Behaviour problems and the teacher'. In Charlton, T. and David, K. (eds) *Managing Misbehaviour*, ch. 2. London: Macmillan.

Davies, G. (1983) An introduction to life and social skills training. *Journal of the Association of Workers for Maladjusted Children 1* (1) (Spring).

DES (1990) Letter to LEAs: Working together for the Protection of children from Abuse: procedures within the Education Service (20 July).

Dowling, E. and Osborne, E. (eds) (1985) *The Family and the School: A Joint Systems Approach to Problems with Children*. London: Routledge & Kegan Paul.

Egan, G. (1982) *The Skilled Helper*. USA: Booksco.

Elliott, M. (1985) *Preventing Child Sexual Assault, A Practical Guide to Talking with Children*. Child Assault Prevention Programme. London: Bedford Square Press.

Elliott, M. (ed.) (1991) *Bullying: A Practical Guide for Schools*. York: Longman.

Elliott, M./KIDSCAPE (1990) *Stop Bullying!* Kidscape, World Trade Centre, Europe House, London E1 9AA.

Elton, R. (Chair) (1989) *Discipline in Schools*. London: HMSO.

*Fontana, D. (1985) *Classroom Control*. London: Methuen/British Psychological Society.

Ford, J., Mongon, D. and Whelan, M. (1982) *Special Education and Social Control: Invisible Disasters*. London: Routledge & Kegan Paul.

Galloway, D., Ball, T., Blomfield, D. and Seyd, R. (1982) *Schools and Disruptive Pupils*. London: Longman.

Galvin, P., Mercer, S. and Costa, P. (1990) *Building a Better Behaved School*. York: Longman.

*Galvin, P. and Singleton, R. (1981) *Behaviour Problems: A System of Management*. Windsor: NFER-Nelson.

*Hanko, G. (1985) *Special Needs in Ordinary Classrooms*. Oxford: Basil Blackwell.

Hargreaves, D., Hester, S. and Mellor, F. (1975) *Deviance in Classrooms*. London: Routledge & Kegan Paul.

*Harris, S. (1983) *Families of the Developmentally Disabled*. Oxford: Pergamon.

*Harrop, A. (1983) *Behaviour Modification in the Classroom*. London: Hodder & Stoughton.

Hartup, W. (1978) 'Children and their friends'. In McGurk, H. (ed.), *Issues in Childhood Social Development*. London: Methuen.

Hegarty, S. (1982) Integration and the comprehensive school. *Educational Review*, Special issue 14. Birmingham: University of Birmingham, Faculty of Education.

*Herbert, M. (1981) *Behavioural Treatment of Problem Children: A Practice Manual*. London: Academic Press.

*Hopson, B. and Scally, M. (1981) *Lifeskills Teaching*. London: McGraw-Hill.

Hughes, J. (1988) *Cognitive Behaviour Therapy with Children in Schools*. Oxford: Pergamon.

Imich, A. and Jefferies, K. (1989) Management of lunchtime behaviour. *Support for Learning* 4 (1) (February).

Kolvin, I., Garside, R.F., Nicol, A.R., Macmillan, A., Wolstenholme, F. and Leitch, I.M. (1981) *Help Starts Here: The Maladjusted Child in the Ordinary School*. London: Tavistock Publications.

Lane, D. (1986) 'Promoting positive behaviour in the classroom'. In Tattum, op. cit.

Laslett, R. (1977) *Educating Maladjusted Children*. London: Crosby, Lockwood, Staples.

*Leach, D. and Raybould, E. (1977) *Learning and Behaviour Difficulties in Schools*. London: Open Books.

Lloyd-Smith, M. (1984) *Disrupted Schooling: The Growth of the Special Unit*. London: Murray.

*Lovitt, T. (1984) *Tactics for Teaching*. Columbus, OH: Charles E. Merrill.

McGregor McMaster, J. (1982) *Methods in Social and Educational Caring*. Aldershot: Gower.

Maher, P. (ed.) (1987) *Child Abuse: The Educational Perspective*. Oxford: Basil Blackwell.

Merrett, F. (1985) *Encouragement Works Better than Punishment*. Birmingham: Positive Products/University of Birmingham, Faculty of Education.

Mongon, D., Hart, S. with Ace, S. and Rawlings, A. (1989) *Improving Classroom Behaviour: New Directions for Teachers and Pupils*. London: Cassell.

Morgan, R. (1984) *Behavioural Treatments with Children*. London: Heinemann.

Morris, K. and Kratochwill, T. (1983) *The Practice of Child Therapy*. Oxford: Pergamon.

Mortimore, P., Davies, J., Varlaam, A. and West, A. (1983) *Behaviour Problems in Schools: An Evaluation of Support Centres*. London: Croom Helm.

Murgatroyd, S. (ed.) (1980) *Helping the Troubled Child: Inter-Professional Case Studies*. London: Harper & Row.

Nelson-Jones, R. (1988) *Practical Counselling and Helping Skills*. 2nd edn. London: Cassell.

Northumberland LEA (1989) *Let's Get On* (Social Skills training).

*Nottingham University (1980) *Nottingham Class Management Observation Schedule*. School of Education, Teacher Education Project.

*Ollendick, T. and Hersen, M. (1984) *Child Behavioural Assessment*. Oxford: Pergamon.

*Open University (1981) *Living with Children 5–10: A Parents' Guide*. London: Harper & Row/Open University Press.

Oxford Polytechnic (1990) *School Discipline: A Study Pack*. Oxford: Education Method Unit in association with L. B. Bexley.

Parton, N. (1985) *The Politics of Child Abuse*. Basingstoke: Macmillan.

Pollard, A. (1985) *The Social World of the Primary School*. Eastbourne: Holt, Rinehart & Winston.

Porter, R. (ed.) (1984) *Child Sexual Abuse within the Family*. London: Tavistock Publications.

Poteet, J. (1973) *Behaviour Modification: A Practical Guide for Teachers*. London: University of London Press.

*Raymond, J. (1985) *Implementing Pastoral Care in Schools*. Beckenham: Croom Helm.

Rhodes, W. and Paul, J. (1978) *Emotionally Disturbed and Deviant Children*. Englewood Cliffs, NJ: Prentice-Hall.

*Robertson, J. (1989) *Effective Classroom Control*, 2nd ed. London: Hodder & Stoughton.

Rogers, B. (1991) *You Know the Fair Rule*. York: Longman.

Ross, C. and Ryan, A. (1990) *Can I Stay In Today, Miss? Improving the School Playground*. Stoke-on-Trent: Trentham Books.

Rubin, Z. (1980) *Children's Friendships*. London: Fontana.

Rutter, M. (1965) Classification and categorisation in child psychiatry. *Journal of Child Psychology and Psychiatry* 6, 71–83.

Rutter, M. (1975) *Helping Troubled Children*. Harmondsworth: Penguin.

Rutter, M., Tizard, J. and Whitmore, K. (1970) *Education, Health and Behaviour*. Harlow: Longman.

Schwartz, S. and Johnson, J. (1981) *Psychopathology of Childhood*. Oxford: Pergamon.

Shepherd, M., Oppenheim, B. and Mitchell, S. (1971) *Childhood Behaviour and Mental Health*. London: University of London Press.

Sisterson, D. (1983) Counselling in the primary school. *British Psychological Society, Education Section Review* 7 (2).

Smith, P. (ed.) (1986) *Children's Play: Research Developments and Practical Applications*. London: Gordon & Breach.

Smith, P. and Thompson, D. (1991) *Practical Approaches to Bullying*. London: David Fulton.

*Spence, S. and Shepherd, G. (eds) (1983) *Development in Social Skills Training*. London: Academic Press.

*Sprick, R. (1981) *The Solution Book*. Henley-on-Thames: Science Research Associates.

Stott, D. (no date) *Bristol Social Adjustment Guides*. London: University of London Press.

*Stott, D. (1982) *Helping the Maladjusted Child*. Milton Keynes: Open University Press.

Stott, D., Marston, N. and Neill, S. (1975) *Taxonomy of Behaviour Disturbance*. London: University of London Press.

Tattum, D. (ed.) (1986) *Management of Disruptive Pupil Behaviour in Schools*. Chichester: John Wiley.

Tattum, D. and Herbert, G. (1990) *Bullying: A Positive Response*. Cardiff: South Glamorgan Institute of Higher Education.

Tattum, D. and Lane, D. (eds) (1989) *Bullying in Schools*. Stoke-on-Trent: Trentham Books.

*Thacker, J. (1985) Extending developmental groupwork to junior/middle schools: an Exeter project. *Pastoral Care* (February).

*TIPS, *The Macmillan Teacher Information Pack* (1985) (Dawson, R. *et al.*) Basingstoke: Macmillan Education.

Topping, K. (1983) *Educational Systems for Disruptive Adolescents*. London: Croom Helm.

Topping, K. (1986) 'Consultative enhancement of school-based action'. In Tattum, op. cit.

Tweddle, D. (ed.) (1986) *Preventive Approaches to Disruption*. Basingstoke: Macmillan.

Underwood Report (1955) *Report of the Committee on Maladjusted Children*. London: HMSO.

*Walker, J. and Shea, T. (1984) *Behavior Management, A Practical Approach for Educators*. St Louis, MO: C. V. Mosby.

Watkins, C. and Wagner, P. (1987) *School Discipline: A Whole-school Approach*. Oxford: Basil Blackwell.

*Westmacott, E. V. S. and Cameron, R. J. (1981) *Behaviour Can Change*. Basingstoke: Macmillan.

Wheldall, K. and Merrett, F. (1984) *BATPACK*. Birmingham: Positive Products/University of Birmingham.

Wheldall, K., Merrett, F. and Glynn, T. (eds) (1986) *Behaviour Analysis in Educational Psychology*. Beckenham: Croom Helm.

Williams, P. (1977) *Children and Psychologists*. London: Hodder & Stoughton.

Wiltshire LEA (1989) *Wiltshire Adjustment Support Preparation* (WASP).

Wolfendale, S. (1988) *The Parental Contribution to Assessment*. Developing Horizons no. 10. Stratford-upon-Avon: National Council for Special Education.

Wolfendale, S. (1990) *Involving Parents in Behaviour Management: A Whole-school Approach*. In Scherer, M., Gersch, I. and Fry, L. (eds) *Meeting Disruptive Behaviour: Assessment, Intervention and Partnership*. London: Macmillan.

Wolfendale, S. and Bryans, T. (1989) *Managing Behaviour: A Practical Framework for Schools*. Stafford: National Association for Remedial Education.

Wolfendale, S, Fox, M. and Hayes, S. (eds) (1991) *Managing Behaviour: Implications for Educational Psychologists of the Elton Report*. Report of a Working Party, available from Psychology Dept, Polytechnic of East London, Romford Road, London E15 4LZ.

*Wood, J. (1984) *Adapting Instruction for the Mainstream*. Columbus, OH: Charles E. Merrill.

Woolfe, R. (1981) 'Maladjustment in the context of local authority decision-making'. In Barton, L. and Tomlinson, S. (eds) *Special Education: Policy, Practice and Social Issues*. London: Harper & Row.

Organisation of classroom and school: collective responsibility in action

The potential of teamwork where expertise within primary schools is harnessed towards collectively providing for special needs has been mentioned at strategic points in previous chapters. This chapter deals with the various components of teamwork and liaison and selects a number of key angles or facets to demonstrate different responsibilities intrinsic to teamwork. These will include:

- the classroom
- curriculum
- staffing
- links with special schools
- liaison with support services
- liaison with parents, and governors.

Overall, it is the vision of a network of educational and support services to meet special educational needs that guides and informs the chapter.

THE SCHOOL AS A SYSTEM

Increasing attention is being paid to the features, both abstract and concrete, that comprise and define any institution. It is acknowledged that buildings, space, room layout (visible features), as well as personnel deployment, interaction between personnel, hierarchies, communication links, organisation (less immediately visible features), are profoundly influential upon the efficient working of any institution or organisation.

Borrowing some basic concepts from engineering, several educational psychologists in the United Kingdom have described the application of systems approaches to their work in schools (Burden, 1981). It is increasingly common for educational psychologists to broaden the base of their practice by examining the 'system' and 'subsystems' of a school in order to understand the contexts in which children find themselves daily (Figg and Ross, 1981). One of the central themes in headteachers' management training is, of course, organisation and management of the whole school. This necessitates taking a total or 'macro' perspective and applying a number of techniques, including diagrammatic ones, to help depict, describe and explain the complex networks that comprise an organisation.

Current writings within the field of special needs embrace these broader perspectives and acknowledge that it is essential to explore them in planning and managing school-based special needs provision as the 'micro' aspects of individual children's progress (Thomas and Feiler, 1988).

ECOLOGICAL PERSPECTIVES AND APPLICATIONS

Reference has already been made in Chapters 2 and 4 to ecological perspectives that have conceptual links with systems approaches. Appendix 5 contains a description of ecological intervention, the technique of 'eco-mapping', provides several examples, and gives references for further reading. The potential of these approaches as part of broad-based assessment, which includes contributions from significant people in a child's life, including him or herself, has hardly been explored in any depth in Britain. One example where it was explored, within a social services context, is described in Appendix 5.

TEAMWORK

The introductory discussion above illuminates some principles of co-operative working. These principles are now outlined in general terms.

Collective responsibility for meeting children's learning and other needs in primary settings will be executed by different personnel, singly or in combinations, at any one time. Duties of key members of a designated team will doubtless be allocated as an integral part of a school's special needs policy (see Chapter 7); yet it is important for all members of staff of any one school to:

- acknowledge the Warnock Report view that at any one time in any class there will be several children with special educational needs (one in five is, of course, the notional average based on survey evidence)
- accept their individual responsibility towards meeting children's special needs.

The discussion in Chapter 1 aimed to represent what appears to be a growing consensus that the educational needs of some children are not best served by a siphoning-off of teaching expertise into remedial spheres that are kept segregated from mainstream curriculum and the hub of school activity. Since designated special needs (see Chapter 1 for definitions) cannot and should not be viewed in isolation from all children's distinctive learning and other needs, it follows that all teachers have to maintain some surveillance of whether these are being met. The National Curriculum Council guidelines 1, 2 and 3 (NCC, 1989a, 1989b, 1990) reinforce this view.

The all encompassing philosophy of the 'whole-school' approach to integration is examined by Thomas and Jackson (1986). Their article does not minimise what is involved in working towards organisational change at this 'macro' level. This chapter now aims to explore selected areas of teamwork and to look at current views as to how collective responsibility can work in practice.

Readers who want case study examples of teamwork in operation within integrated settings can find these described in more detail in Hegarty, Pocklington and Lucas (1982), in the appendix of Booth and Potts (1983), in Hodgson, Clunies-Ross and Hegarty (1984) and in the factsheets published by the Centre for Studies on Integration in Education (address in references).

PLANNING AND MANAGING THE CURRICULUM AS A CORPORATE ACTIVITY

Specific responsibilities for core and foundation subject areas, e.g. literacy, numeracy, primary science, music, art and craft, drama, PE and others, may or may not be within the generic remit of class teachers and/or subject specialists or responsibility posts in any one primary school. However, as the Fish Report (1985) points out, 'A school's curriculum, derived from the agreed aims of the school, should reflect the cultural, social and racial diversity of the pupils who attend it and the community it serves' (p. 57, para. 2.7.7).

Therefore, the collective responsibility of all the teachers within the school is to 'have a clear idea of progression in all aspects of the curriculum and to use this as a framework for evaluating individual progress' (p. 57, 2.7.6).

The Report continues

> It is on this basis for assessing the progress of all children that it is possible to become aware of children who have special educational needs, either because they are making no progress or because their progress is significantly less than that of other children. (p. 57, 2.7.6)

The setting of teaching objectives for each child follows within this model of a 'curriculum framework'. Echoing the particular theme of the present chapter, the Fish Report goes on later to affirm, in discussing curriculum,

> in the organisation and management of a wide range of activities including team teaching and collaborative learning are an essential basis for meeting the variety of individual needs of children in primary schools. (p. 184, 3.17.21)

In Chapter 1 of this book a theoretical stance was first sketched out that sought to achieve a rapprochement between 'good' (tried and true?) principles of primary practice and 'best' or proven practice within remedial/special education.

Some of the proven, effective features of primary curriculum practice quoted by Fish and his colleagues (Fish, 1985a, ch. 7) appear to be synonymous with 'good' teaching practice in the area of special needs. Should we be surprised? Perhaps now, after creating and then nurturing red herrings in the form of segregated provision, we are rediscovering that some sound pedagogical principles do apply to all children. As we shall see below, the ORACLE researchers uncovered some factors that appeared to make for effective teaching/learning. They went on to make recommendations that would, they felt, benefit all the children within any one class with a broad spread of individual competence and a variety of 'special' learning needs.

Textbooks on primary curriculum, content and method, have traditionally dealt with all children, simply by not explicitly categorising groups of children. It may now be timely to return to these texts on behalf of those children with designated special needs – a child on a statement of special needs; one with sensory handicap, or with moderate learning difficulties; a child with epilepsy on controlled medication and under nursing surveillance; a child with a cluster of conditions needing special attention. Campbell (1985) in fact discusses the notion of collective responsibility in staking out the territory for his book in these words:

> if teachers participate in some explicitly collaborative action to recreate the curriculum in their school, rather than acting as individuals to receive it, they may move closer to accepting collective responsibility for the curriculum overall in the school, as well as for its application in their own classrooms. (p. 3)

Campbell goes on to set out his vision of the 'collegial' primary school which, he avers, is 'a projection from empirical reality', not a description of it at present. His views represent an ideal that is strikingly akin to the model of collective responsibility for special and all needs contained in this book. Campbell's 'collegial' model is predicated on the two values of 'teacher collaboration and subject expertise' (p. 152).

Turning now to another text on primary education, we can see that Alexander (1984) justifies his attention to the teacher's role thus:

> because it is the teacher . . . who defines the child in child-centred . . . approach, who defines children's attributes, states what their needs are, predicts their potential and evaluates their achievement. It could be argued, then, that knowing oneself as a teacher is one of the basic prerequisites for true child-centredness. (p. 2)

Here the child-centred view of primary education is reaffirmed but Alexander goes on to examine a fallacy concerned with child-centred education, namely that it has to be exclusively focused on the child. He examines the feasibility of a 'child-centred' primary curriculum that is rooted within societal perspectives (Stonier, 1982) and says 'using societal analysis as the starting point he [Stonier] effectively avoids the individual/society polarisation which inevitably ensues from the exclusively child-centred position' (p. 33).

Alexander's analysis of the curriculum has much to offer anyone coming from the direction of remedial/special education who wishes to embrace the broadest possible conception of integration. His critique of many conventional assumptions and received wisdom within education are a wincing reminder that segregated philosophies are morally untenable. Further, his view accords with this author's that the whole psycho-pedagogical basis of teacher's 'knowledge' of children, of their learning potential, their unique circumstances, needs to be challenged.

The ideas put forward in Chapter 3 and 4 of this book do represent what we think we know at the present time about how to meet children's learning needs and deal with emotional development and social adjustment. But there is much work to be done still to reconcile individual teaching approaches with theories of pedagogy that can actually be empirically tested and proven.

My aspiration, then, is to effect a synthesis between the traditions of primary and remedial/special education. In itself this could be a static aim, one that does not move us on far enough to cope with education imperatives of the 1990s and beyond. However, the fusion that is envisaged is actually to be able to offer curricula of relevance to all children – who collectively come from and represent a diversity of cultural, religious, and ethnic backgrounds. Thus, the moral imperative, in Alexander's words, is 'that curriculum discourse ought to incorporate and synthesize perspectives on children, knowledge, culture and pedagogy' (p. 47).

How do these words read now, in the context of the National Curriculum? Is the Curriculum a straitjacket, a constraint to the realisation of these aspirations (Bash and Coulby, 1989) or is it a liberating force that allows for such pluralist aims to be incorporated into children's education? Pring (1989) observes that the quality of the curriculum 'depends to some extent on the assurance of long-term funding for a school' (p. 65) and goes on to suggest that quality as well as consistency and continuity between schools would and could not be guaranteed in a system that includes a range of private independent, grant-maintained, and LEA-maintained schools (and see discussion in Ball, 1990).

Evidently the continued access of children with special educational needs to *all* aspects of the school curriculum is correspondingly at risk in such a scenario, a point reiterated by Hayes (1991).

So our present reality is not only our ERA-dominated educational culture, but the legacy of ambivalent attitudes on the part of teachers towards handicap and disability (see Chapter 1). All these factors make the task of agreeing corporate responsibility for organising curriculum opportunities for children with special needs that much more of a challenge.

ORGANISING THE CLASSROOM: TEAMWORK AND CO-OPERATION

It is clear from contemporary texts on primary education as well as from trends in thinking in special needs that the view is increasingly disfavoured that the class teacher should be expected to shoulder the daily and entire responsibility for curriculum planning, execution and management; and that one person is capable of providing a total educational experience for all the children in his or her charge. The dangers of looking inward, what Alexander describes as the 'cosy, privatised equilibrium of "my class"' (p. 215) and the commensurate guilt at not achieving self-directed personal teaching goals, can be averted or at least reduced by undertaking 'collective analysis of shared issues and problems' (Alexander, 1984, p. 216; see also Alexander, Rose and Woodhead, 1992).

The co-operative team approach can nowhere be better put into effect than in classrooms and there is increasing evidence that corporate teaching can be the most effective way of ensuring that each child receives his or her rightful share of teacher's attention and teaching time, working solo, in combinations, in small groups in the whole class.

The question of how best to organise children within the classroom has always attracted debate but with little corresponding empirical evidence as to prevailing custom.

The ORACLE study (Galton, Simon and Croll, 1980; Galton and Simon, 1980) provides harder data, from which the researchers conclude 'that the whole issue of the purpose and organisation of group work in the primary school classroom requires a great deal more attention than it has had to date' (Galton *et al.*, p. 161).

1. Involving pupils in collaborative work

It seems that there is more potential for effective learning through small group collaboration than has yet been fully realised, for the evidence suggests that, within the small-group clusters so characteristic of primary classrooms, children tended to work on their own, in parallel rather than in co-operation.

Recently there has been particular notice paid to the benefits of co-operative learning (Reason, Rooney and Roffe, 1987) as opposed to the static nature of merely ensuring physical proximity. Co-operative learning, at primary and secondary levels, can be defined as groupwork with any one (or more) of these aims: collaboration on a specific project, i.e. shared learning; mutual co-operation and assistance; learning to work in parallel as well as solo; incorporating social interaction with attention to the task in hand. Projects have taken place in infant, junior and also in secondary schools in which pupils' and teachers' attitudes to co-operative group work have been explored. These studies have indicated that there are several issues that need resolution as a prerequisite for the incorporation of group work into the school, such as sympathy for and acceptance of the ideas by other staff members, if not active involvement from them, and the probable need for social engineering by teachers. (These issues are discussed in Kutnick, 1988 and by Slavin, 1990.) There are implications here for peer tutoring, which has been explored in the realm of reading (see end of Chapter 3).

The planning requisites that such studies identify raise questions about staff–pupil ratios as well as the underlying issues previously raised concerning sharing responsibility. Galton, Simon and Croll (1980) are of the opinion that maximum class size in British primary schools should be 20; this number would allow for effective reaching of all the children in a truly mixed-ability class and would promote co-operative learning.

Cohering with these research findings are those of special needs-focused investigations into classroom organisation and staff deployment.

2. Room management

The area of severe learning difficulties has been a pacesetter in demonstrating the effectiveness of 'room management' (RM) techniques via the provision of other staff in one classroom, each of whom have explicit jobs for an agreed period of time during a day (McBrien and Weightman, 1980; Farrell, 1985). During this 'activity' period, which could be about an hour long, specific roles are allotted to staff in the classroom:

1. *Individual helper* who concentrates on taking individual children for short periods of time.
2. *Activity manager* who looks after the work of the rest of the children, the aim being to keep the children engaged on the task in hand.
3. *Mover* who aims to maintain flow in the classroom by relieving the activity manager and individual helper from distracting events. The mover can deal with the various contingencies that crop up – coping with interruptions, sharpening pencils.

The EDY (Education of the Developmentally Young) staff training programme, which pioneered RM techniques in the United Kingdom, derives from behavioural principles, is very stringent and requires a several-day training course with certification at the end. Thousands of staff from special schools have now been trained in EDY techniques and, as with PORTAGE (see Chapter 3), success can be measured by children's productivity. Children's output within EDY would be one of the criteria for gauging how effective this kind of time and motion can be.

Although the staff–pupil ratios are far higher in special schools, there are nevertheless implications for the adoption of RM techniques in mainstream schools that bear examination. Thomas (1985) considered the deployment of additional personnel, including volunteers, and in one primary school tried out the effectiveness of allotting RM roles (see above) to two parents and one ancillary helper. He acknowledges methodological and other limitations to his study, yet concludes 'the results obtained are attributable mainly to the advantages of RM accruing from specification of role'.

How realistic would it be to envisage an RM type of approach within primary classrooms, so that each child receives some structured, intensive teaching and support during a school day? In principle there seem to be evident pedagogic advantages in having extra personnel with clearly identified tasks who would corporately bring about learning gains by:

- giving immediate feedback, knowledge of results
- swiftly applying correction procedures to 'errors'
- promptly reiterating instructions
- facilitating self-monitoring by pupils

- ensuring that short-term sessional or daily goals are met
- redirecting pupils to alternative or related tasks
- flexibly matching materials and resources to child
- anticipating and dealing with behaviour
- maintaining motivation and on-task behaviour by frequent attention, interest, encouragement, and support

The physical aspects of classroom management are important corollaries of human management, such as arrangement of furniture, acoustics, lighting (Hodgson, Clunies-Ross and Hegarty, 1984, ch. 10), organising the 'learning station' (Wood, 1984), and seating arrangements (Stratford). Whilst these may seem rather obvious considerations, the point here is that these too have to be articulated and worked into an overall plan of classroom management.

3. Staffing and support

Galton *et al.* (see above) are unequivocal in their opinion that children should have a better deal in terms of teachers' attention. Readers are reminded that in Chapter 3 (pp. 54–5) Bloom's five 'alterable variables' were listed *vis-à-vis* their applicability in primary classrooms. In particular, no. 1, 'Available time versus time-on-task', and no. 4, 'Teachers versus teaching', are compatible with the view that, at present, class teachers do not have enough opportunities to utilise sound instructional principles and by virtue of having large groups have to teach in a blunt, undifferentiated way. Even when they work with small groups, teachers frequently have to attend to many other distractions in the classroom.

Booth (1983) described the deployment of 'remedial specialists' in the Grampian region who acted as consultants to other members of staff and also worked alongside the class teacher. Ferguson and Adams (1985) assessed the advantages and limitations of the Grampian scheme. They were conscious of the drawbacks to maintaining the term 'remedial', acknowledging that we are still very much in an evolving situation:

> one way . . . is to make provision for both to work in the same classroom at the same time. This is a potentially useful way of integrating remedial education with the school curriculum . . . helping class and remedial teachers to improve their understanding of each other's problems and special skills. (p. 99)

Hodgson *et al.* cited schools (without naming them) in the NFER study that utilised second teachers and ancillaries to provide support in mainstream classes, working perhaps with one pupil (possibly a child whose statement of needs explicitly calls for extra teaching help and prescribes the extent and nature of that help); with small groups of designated special needs children; with mixed groups. A useful summary of this part of the NFER study is provided by Clunies-Ross (1984).

Hockley (1985) gave a firsthand account of having been a support teacher in primary and secondary settings, and identifies and explains these elements of the classroom-based aspects of her role: flexibility; observation; problem classification and suggestions for different approaches; monitoring; consultations with staff.

The label of 'support teacher' may not be the most appropriate one to use – Hart (1986) pointed out that the term might imply a less than equal relationship with support ancillary to real specialists and, further, perpetuate the idea of 'remedial' being tangential to the body of the curriculum. She suggested that a broader definition of special educational need to encompass prevention would validly allow support teachers to work with other teachers to develop a curriculum 'capable of meeting a progressively wider diversity of needs' (p. 58). Thus, support teachers could play a significant part in 'promoting good teaching for all children within the general curriculum', and 'working in partnership with subject teachers, support teachers could . . . try out a variety of different approaches and monitor their effectiveness in catering for all needs within the class'.

The Inner London Education Authority's IBIS (Inspectors Based in Schools) scheme, begun in 1986, was designed to eliminate the demarcation between ordinary and special/remedial education by giving a brief to each school-based inspector to 'help to improve the quality of education and the achievement of pupils'.

The above discussion summarises the situation around the early to mid-1980s and draws no distinction between designated special needs teachers based full-time in one school and part of the school staff and 'visiting' support/advisory teachers who have a patch of schools and operate from a central LEA service. These two types of provision have developed in parallel in recent years and it is worth briefly charting the trends and one or two of the issues.

WITHIN-SCHOOL SUPPORT: ROLE OF THE SPECIAL NEEDS TEACHER

As Dyer noted (1988), the very term 'support' has been taken on board, is used as an alternative synonym for 'remedial', though the semantics may differ, and has a number of connotations. He goes on to examine critically forms of support to pupils and foresees that the change of nomenclature itself could and should encourage attitude change towards special needs and learning difficulties.

However, a survey undertaken by Jeffs (1987) demonstrated that the role of the school-based support teacher can be equivocal if undefined clearly. A number of ambiguities concerned with status and influence emerged, though in his conclusions Jeffs was clear that whilst day-to-day responsibility should be vested in the designated teacher, special educational needs is a 'whole school, full staff responsibility'.

In fact the uncertain balance, power and place of the special educational needs teacher-co-ordinator is highlighted by the arrival of the National Curriculum and the principles of entitlement of all children to full access to all curriculum opportunities. Discussion and debate as to the continuing and future role within such a context and LMS arrangements has taken place on the pages of the journal *Support for Learning* (Dyson, 1990; Butt, 1991). At least, both writers agree on the fact that a new title, that of 'effective learning consultant' may:

- maintain the post-holder as a key member of staff, with a legitimate role to 'promote positive learning' (see Chapter 3 above);
- reduce the threat of such a post being marginalised; and
- reinforce the 'whole school' approach to effective learning.

SUPPORTING THE SCHOOL FROM OUTSIDE: ROLE OF THE ADVISORY TEACHER

Provision of outside support has been a feature of remedial education for many years and the model of the peripatetic teacher has perpetuated. What distinguishes the present from the erstwhile role are these features:

- disuse of the term 'remedial'
- focus on learning support and skill-development rather than on reading only
- a greater array of teaching approaches backed up by a range of materials
- improved inservice training/greater expertise.

The evolution of local provision to an LEA support service is described by Drew (1990), who illustrates a number of features which include the pointers listed just above. Clearly in many LEAs the service now has higher status than the old-style Remedial Service did, as is evinced by the creation of the post of Head of Service and the fact that a national organisation entitled SENSSA (Special Educational Needs Support Services Association), has been formed (1991) to represent the interests of teachers in support services. Its aims include: raising awareness of its services; offering advice; facilitating professional development;

publishing members' work; developing an advocacy role on behalf of children and their families. Members are concerned over the future security of such services under LMS and over the threat that delegation could pose to children with special needs.

SUPPORTING CLASS TEACHERS: THE GROWTH OF WELFARE ASSISTANTS

One phenomenon of the 1980s was the increasing appointment of personnel working with, alongside and co-operatively with teachers who shared a brief for children with special needs, and particularly those with statements of special need. Mostly known as welfare assistants, but also as ancillaries, auxiliaries, teacher aides and non-teaching assistants, they traditionally worked in nursery and infant schools and are increasingly found working with older children with special needs. Usually they have been women and untrained for such work unless they happen to be trained teachers, nurses, etc.

As their numbers have grown and as their input into special needs has increased so have their training and support needs begun to receive attention, albeit on a hugely variable scale and extent.

One of the first training packs was devised by Oxfordshire LEA (OPTIS) in the mid-1980s and there is a more recent set of materials, SAINTS (Special Assistants Inservice Training Scheme), produced by Wiltshire LEA (1989) and described by one of its authors, Clayton (1990), in a preliminary survey that provides data on the previous experience and training of 100 welfare assistants who responded to a questionnaire. More or less all had some related or relevant prior training or experience, which also, of course, illuminated their interest in becoming welfare assistants in this area. The data also highlight the need for them to receive inservice training and support.

Finally, in this section on classroom-based personnel, a word about using parents as volunteer 'aides'. The potential of parental assistance within schools has been explored in the area of reading (see Chapter 2), but far less in other curriculum areas. Without abusing their goodwill and the limited amount of time parents can offer, it would be part of the notion of collective responsibility to approach and negotiate with parents as to what they could contribute – working with groups on reading, language, maths workshops and other curriculum areas; acting as an identified 'helper' as in the RM model; providing one-to-one assistance on an individual teaching programme for a child whose statement of needs prescribes clear teaching and learning objectives. 'Parents as educators' can then become reality.

UNITS WITHIN SCHOOLS

The above discussion has concentrated on co-operative teaching within children's 'home base', their classrooms, since, as the diagrammatic web (see p. 103) shows, integration is rooted within classrooms. Much has been written on varieties of integration, though purists would maintain that any form of withdrawal is an erosion of interaction principles. If a school can demonstrate that all the children in a given class receive instruction at some time outside the classroom (which of course they do) and can thereby prove that no child or group is singled out and stigmatised in this way, then withdrawal to units, resource areas, etc. is tenable.

The reason for making reference to provision that supplements, rather than supplants, mainline classroom-based teaching is that, again, it is a requisite of pre-planned teamwork that access to specialist equipment, other resources and materials is effected on the basis of stringently defined criteria. The summary of the NFER study (Hodgson, Clunies-Ross and Hegarty, 1984) presupposed in fact that, in order to meet the special needs of children with particular disabilities, there had to be access to specialist teaching and equipment (see below).

Literature from the Warnock Report onwards, and including the NFER studies, has shown variations on the theme of integration in terms of units and withdrawal arrangements. Changing practice was encapsulated by Selfe and Gray (1985) who, in describing their experience of unit provision within one rural area of a large county, averred that units within school provision was en route towards full functional integration: 'They are, in fact, better placed . . . than are segregated special schools since opportunities for integration and a wider curriculum are on hand' (p. 123).

Teachers are not, then, in a position to 'disown' children with special needs or their responsibility towards them and they have the opportunity to broaden their own expertise (Galloway, 1990).

LINKS BETWEEN MAINSTREAM AND SPECIAL SCHOOLS

Despite official commitment to integration enshrined in the 1981 Education Act, there has been no consensus as to how to implement it nor an agreed timescale. It has become evident, since the Act came into force on 1 April 1983, that LEAs vary enormously in their thinking and practice. Many do not provide a written account of their plans, some are still deliberating via working parties and consultative documents.

For all LEAs, however, the implications of LMS for integration are sober reality factors, irrespective of what progress has been made (a survey by Swann, based on 1990 figures, indicates an increase in integrated provision by approximately 40–45 per cent and in segregated provision by around 10–15 per cent of LEAs between 1982 and 1990 (report available from CSIE).

And yet, on the ground, professional staff are directly responding to the Act, and ensuring that the demarcation between remedial/special/mainstream is increasingly blurred, as Warnock recommended (see Chapter 1).

Since many of the links between mainstream and special schools are occurring at practitioner level, mostly routinely within LEAs, documentation chronicling these developments is inadequate. However, whilst detailed survey evidence is lacking, the literature does provide some portents as to trends and how these arrangements may work. There are a few prescriptions (Brennan, 1982), documented examples (Hallmark and Dessent, 1982; Hallmark, 1983) and descriptive data.

As with units-within-school provision, mainstream–special school liaison may in time be seen to have been a transitional arrangement en route to integration. But what is not and cannot yet be resolved on financial as well as ideological grounds is whether or not special schools will wither away, will become resource centres of expertise and technology, transporting them to mainstream (Dessent, 1984; Dodman, 1985), or will be retained to provide for 'special care' children.

So what we can know in the short term, pragmatically, is how special/mainstream links can meet children's needs, can rationalise local resources, can ensure sharing and pooling knowledge and concern on behalf of children. In other words, collective responsibility extends beyond the frontiers of any one school, as Figure 5.1 (p. 103) illustrates.

SCHOOLS AND SUPPORT SERVICES

A recurring theme in this volume is the need for people who work with and on behalf of children to understand the bases and intentions of each other's contribution. Multidisciplinary teamwork is seen to be one of the cornerstones of the 1981 Education Act as well as being within the broader context of special needs (DES, 1989).

There are examples of inservice training organised by DHA (District Health Authority) personnel directed to teachers to acquaint them with the medical and physical implications of disability. Likewise there have been courses run by LEA personnel for others in health and social services in the 1981 Education Act and educational aspects of special needs (and see Chapter 6).

Courses and workshops for parents and professionals provide a forum for interdisciplinary acquaintance that can lead to joint work. PORTAGE has provided opportunities for professionals who never worked together previously to interact and pool their expertise.

Again, then, on the ground there has been evidence of developing networks of communication between agencies, some of these confounding the critics who are pessimistic about the ease with which professionals can divest themselves of their *amour propre*, relinquish some of their mystique, and bring their arcane jargon and rituals to public scrutiny (Potts, 1985). Recent inter-departmental guidelines such as those on child abuse (see Chapter 4) and the 1989 Children Act have also galvanised inter-agency co-operative endeavours.

The context for this chapter is the school. Teachers have the right to be far better informed about the relative contributions of the support services. That right is a prerequisite to the formulation of school-based referral procedures and liaison mechanisms. Quicke (1985) expressed the view that support should be defined in terms of mutuality, that is, 'genuine teamwork implies mutual not one-way support' (p. 122). Thomson's helpful list of agencies (1984) was generated as part of a study he made into the special school headteacher's position as a member of a multidisciplinary team and it endorses Quicke's notion of mutuality.

Descriptions of support services, including critiques such as Potts's own trenchant offering (1985), still take a profession-centric standpoint, tending to ignore the contribution of local and national voluntary agencies. Two exceptions are Gliedmann and Roth (1981) and Adams (1986), who clearly perceived that a truly integrated child support system that includes schools is truly community-based and involves parents as equals (Wolfendale, 1983, chapters 8 and 10).

SCHOOLS, THEIR GOVERNING BODIES AND SPECIAL EDUCATIONAL NEEDS

Governors now have significantly increased duties and responsibilities in respect of staffing, including appointments and finance, via the Local Management of Schools mechanisms. Other duties include dealing with grievances and dismissals, and, as part of financial delegation, responsibility for books, equipment and examination fees. A notable shift is the new duty upon governors to ensure that the National Curriculum is delivered properly, which means that they must be knowledgeable about the core and foundation subjects, and aware of programmes of study, attainment targets, and means of assessment, especially SATs.

Special educational needs

Three important new duties were assigned to governors in the 1981 Education Act:

- to use their best endeavours to ensure that children with special needs in their school are receiving an education that caters for them properly;
- to ensure that everyone teaching children with special needs knows about those needs and how they are to be met;
- to ensure that everyone in schools understands the importance of identifying children with special needs and providing for them.

The National Association of Governors and Managers (NAGM) published a paper (1984) that not only explained these duties in some detail but provided lists of questions governors could ask in respect of curriculum facilities and parental and community involvement. An ACE handout (1988) incorporates these duties with ones detailed in the 1986 and 1988 Education Acts in respect of special needs.

Under ERA, governors' duties for special needs are extended, pervasive and no longer discrete, i.e. decision-making on resources, statementing, placement, staffing, use of support services, modification and/or disapplication from the National Curriculum form a part of governors' responsibilities within their overall responsibility for the National Curriculum and finances.

There is, correspondingly, a tremendous onus on LEAs and governing bodies to ensure that the legislation and the duties are understood, interpreted accurately and acted upon. Likewise there are significant pressures for high-quality decision-making which is not unduly influenced or limited by cost factors and other competing demands. Professionals and parents already confronting these issues are aware that in a market economy-dominated education service special needs could once more become a vulnerable area. Thus many parents will be looking to governors to exercise their duties in respect of special needs in a 'morally acceptable' way.

Provision for training governors in the area of special needs is gradually increasing (see Dodd, 1989 and Wolfendale, 1990, for descriptions of local work). In the case of the London Borough of Newham, as described by Wolfendale, there has been a training programme since 1984–85 and schools' governing bodies are expected to have a 'named' special needs link governor with clear functions and also have a special educational needs item on each agenda. Thus the profile of special educational needs is maintained and governors are enabled to support schools in implementing special needs policies.

THE NETWORK OF SERVICES

The tables contained in Chapters 3 and 4 were intended to provide a summary of possibilities for joint working between class teachers, support and advisory teachers, psychologists, parents, and others. The details given in those two charts centred on assessment and intervention approaches that were considered to be amenable to co-operation. One further general example, that of ecological assessment and intervention (ecosystems and ecomapping), was given at the beginning of this chapter to further emphasise such possibilities. Figure 5.1 is an

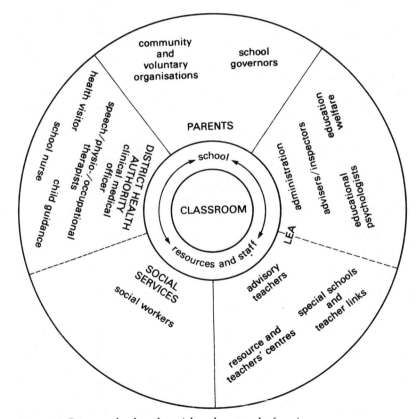

Figure 5.1 Primary schools and special needs: network of services

illustration providing, in circular 'web' form, a representation of the network of services with which this chapter has been concerned. It therefore summarises the elements, in human terms, of collective responsibility.

A number of other contemporary texts echo the theme of co-operation, teamwork and whole-school approach (Sayer, 1985; Thomas and Jackson, 1986). Adams (1986) provides an endorsement of the diagrammatic summary of Figure 5.1 in these words: 'to operate effectively the schools should be at the centre of a network of partnerships' (p. 191).

How responsibilities can be deployed will be further explored in Chapter 7.

REFERENCES

ACE: booklets by Joan Sallis (a) *Questions Governors Ask* (b) *Working Together, Training Exercises* (c) *The School in Its Setting* (d) *The Effective School Governor*. Advisory Centre for Education, 1B Aberdeen Studios, 22 Highbury Grove, London N5 2EA.

ACE (1988) *Governors and Special Needs*. London: Advisory Centre for Education.

Adams, F. (ed.) (1986) *Special Education*. Harlow: Longman/Society of Education Officers.

Alexander, R. (1984) *Primary Teaching*. London: Holt, Rinehart & Winston.

Alexander, R., Rose, J. and Woodhead, C. (1992) *Curriculum Organisation and Classroom Practice in Primary Schools: A Discussion Paper*. London: DES.

Apter, S. (1982) *Troubled Children, Troubled Systems*. Oxford: Pergamon.

Ball, S. (1990) *Politics and Policy-making in Education*. London: Routledge.

Bash, L. and Coulby, D. (1989) *The Education Reform Act: Competition and Control*. London: Cassell.

Booth, T. (1983) 'Integrating special education'. In Booth and Potts, op. cit.

Booth, T. and Potts, P. (eds) (1983) *Integrating Special Educators*. Oxford: Basil Blackwell.

Bowers, A. (ed.) (1984) *Management and the Special School*. Beckenham: Croom Helm.

Brennan, W. (1982) *Changing Special Education*. Milton Keynes: Open University Press.

Bronfenbrenner, U. (1979) *The Ecology of Human Development: Experiments by Nature and Design*. Cambridge, MA: Harvard University Press.

Burden, R. (1981) 'System theory and its relevance to schools'. In Gillham, op. cit.

Butt, N. (1991) A role for the SEN co-ordinator in the 1990s: A reply to Dyson. *Support for Learning* 6 (1) (February).

Campbell, R. J. (1985) *Developing the Primary School Curriculum*. London: Holt, Rinehart & Winston.

Clayton, T. (1990) Welfare assistants: are they equipped for their role? *Support for Learning* 5 (4) (November), 193–9.

Clunies-Ross, L. (1984) Supporting the mainstream teacher. *British Journal of Special Education* 11 (3) (September).

CSIE, 4th Floor, 415 Edgware Road, London NW2 6NB. Tel: (081) 452 8642.

DES (1989) *Assessments and Statements of Special Educational Needs: Procedures within the Education, Health and Social Services*, Circular 22/89. London, DES.

Dessent, A. (1984) 'Special schools and the mainstream'. In Bowers, op. cit.

Dodd, M. (1989) Governor training and special education. *Support for Learning* 5 (1) (February), 13–22.

Dodman, M. (1985) *Delivering support services to mainstream schools: a role for the special school*, Perspectives 15. Exeter: University of Exeter, School of Education.

Drew, D. (1990) From tutorial unit to schools' support service. *Support for Learning* 5 (1) (February), 13–22.

Dyer, C. (1988) Which support? An examination of the term. *Support for Learning* 3 (1) (February).

Dyson, A. (1990) Effective learning consultancy: a future role for special needs co-ordinators. *Support for Learning* 5 (3) (August), 116–28.

Farrell, P. (ed.) (1985) *EDY: Its Impact on Staff Training in Mental Handicap*. Manchester: Manchester University Press.

Ferguson, N. and Adams, M. (1985) 'Assessing the advantages of team teaching in remedial education: the remedial teacher's role'. In Smith, C. (ed.) *New Directions in Remedial Education*. Brighton: Falmer Press.

Figg, J. and Ross, A. (1981) 'Analysing a school system: a practical exercise'. In Gillham, op. cit.

Fish, J. (Chair) (1985a) *Educational Opportunities for All?* London: ILEA.

Fish, J. (1985b) *Special Education: The Way Ahead*. Milton Keynes: Open University Press.

Galloway, D. (1990) 'Interaction with children with special educational needs'. In Rogers and Kutnick, op. cit.

Galton, M. and Simon, B. (eds) (1980) *Progress and Performance in the Primary Classroom*. London: Routledge & Kegan Paul.

Galton, M., Simon, B. and Croll, P. (1980) *Inside the Primary Classroom*. London: Routledge & Kegan Paul.

Gillham, B. (ed.) (1981) *Problem Behaviour in the Secondary School*. London: Croom Helm.

Gliedmann, J. and Roth, W. (1981) 'Parents and professionals'. In Swann, W. (ed.) *The Practice of Special Education*. Oxford: Basil Blackwell/Open University Press.

Hallmark, N. (1983) 'A support service to primary schools'. In Booth and Potts, op. cit.

Hallmark, N. and Dessent, A. (1982) A special education service centre. *British Journal of Special Education* 9 (1).

Hart, S. (1986) In-class support teaching: tackling Fish. *British Journal of Special Education* 13 (2) (June).

Hayes, S. (1991) Too eagerly awaited assessment? *British Journal of Special Education* **18** (2) (June).

Hegarty, S., Pocklington, K. and Lucas, D. (1982) *Integration in Action: Case Studies in the Integration of Pupils with Special Needs.* Windsor: NFER-Nelson.

Hockley, L. (1985) On being a support teacher. *British Journal of Special Education* **12** (1) (March).

Hodgson, A., Clunies-Ross, L. and Hegarty, S. (1984) *Learning Together: Teaching Pupils with Special Educational Needs in the Ordinary School.* Windsor: NFER-Nelson.

Jeffs, A. (1987) *Special Educational Needs: The Role of the 'Designated Teacher' within Primary Schools.* Bristol: Bristol Polytechnic Department of Education.

Kutnick, P. (1988) *Relationships in the Primary School Classroom.* London: Paul Chapman.

McBrien, J. and Weightman, J. (1980) The effect of room management procedures on the engagement of profoundly retarded children. *British Journal of Mental Subnormality* **26** (1), 38–46.

Moses, D. (1985) The end of isolation: link schemes between ordinary and special schools. *Educational and Child Psychology* **2** (3).

NAGM (National Association of Governors and Managers) (1984) Paper no. 5.

NCC (1989a) *Guidance No. 1: A Framework for the Primary Curriculum.* York: National Curriculum Council.

NCC (1989b) *Guidance No. 2: A Curriculum for All: Special Educational Needs in the National Curriculum.* York: National Curriculum Council.

NCC (1990) *Guidance No. 3: The Whole Curriculum.* York: National Curriculum Council.

Open University (1981) *Governing Schools.* Milton Keynes: Open University Press.

Paired Reading Bulletin (1986) no. 2 (Spring). Available from Kirklees School Psychological Service, Oldgate House, 2 Oldgate, Huddersfield, West Yorkshire HD1 6QU.

Potts, P. (1985) 'Training for teamwork'. In Sayer and Jones, op. cit.

Pring, R. (1989) *The New Curriculum.* London: Cassell.

Quicke, J. (1985) 'Initial teacher education and the role of support agencies'. In Sayer and Jones, op. cit.

Reason, R., Rooney, S. and Roffe, M. (1987) Co-operative learning in an infants' school. *Educational and Child Psychology* **4** (3 and 4), 40–9.

Rogers, C. and Kutnick, P. (eds) (1990) *The Social Psychology of the Primary School.* London: Routledge.

SAINTS (1989) prepared by Clayton, T., Moore, S., Parker, R., Powley, V. Trowbridge: Wiltshire Education Dept, Psychological Service.

Sayer, J. (1985) 'A whole-school approach to meeting all needs'. In Sayer and Jones, op. cit.

Sayer, J. and Jones, N. (eds) (1985) *Teacher Training and Special Educational Needs.* Beckenham: Croom Helm.

Selfe, L. and Gray, P. (1985) Units in ordinary schools – a step forward. *British Journal of Special Education* **12** (3) (September).

Sigston, A., Kerfoot, S. and Hogg, R. (1986) *CLASSIC*. Details available from Allan Sigston, Psychology Department, University of East London.

Slavin, R. (1990) 'Co-operative learning'. In Rogers and Kutnick, op. cit., ch. 13.

Stonier, T. (1982) 'Changes in Western society: educational implications'. In yichards, C. (ed.) *New Directions in Primary Education*. Brighton: Falmer Press.

Stratford, R. S. (no date) 'Productivity in the Classroom'. Southampton: University of Southampton, Department of Psychology.

Thomas, G. (1985) Room management in mainstream education. *Educational Research* 27 (3).

Thomas, G. (1986) Integrating personnel in order to integrate children. *Support for Learning* 1 (1) (February).

Thomas, G. and Feiler, A. (eds) (1988) *Planning for Special Needs: A Whole-School Approach*. Oxford: Basil Blackwell.

Thomas, G. and Jackson, B. (1986) The whole-school approach to integration. *British Journal of Special Education* 13 (1) (March).

Thomson, V. (1984) 'Links with other professionals: the head as a multi-disciplinary team member'. In Bowers, op. cit.

Wolfendale, S. (1983) *Parental Participation in Children's Development and Education*. London: Gordon & Breach.

Wolfendale, S., Harskamp, A., Labram, A. and Millward, A. (1990) Governors and special educational needs: a collaborative inservice training programme. *Educational and Child Psychology* 7 (2), 46–54.

Wood, J. (1984) *Adapting Instruction for the Mainstream*. Columbus, OH: Charles E. Merrill.

—6—

Staff development and inservice training: encouraging responsibility

At the heart of all debate on alternative and better ways of meeting children's needs within schools is the issue of teachers themselves and what they bring or do not bring to the educational process. Indeed, what they represent, how they are defined and define themselves are lively components of any debate.

Concern with practitioners who have the care and educational responsibility for children in school is, in this book, equal to concern with children themselves. A multifaceted set of perspectives is advanced, of which teachers' training and expertise to deal with the gamut of children in their charge is paramount.

As we have seen from the previous chapter, Alexander (1984) is in no doubt about the immense responsibility placed upon the teacher. It could be argued that few people are in much doubt about that premise, hence the seemingly never-ending stream of pronouncements from the DES, teaching unions, professional associations and training institutions as to what teaching should consist of and what teachers should 'possess' in the way of skills and qualities.

It may not be possible to escape all charges that, by its very existence, this chapter sets out prescriptions. Indeed the purpose of the book, and of this series, may be seen to be directed towards the changing of attitudes and acquiring of skills on the part of its readers. It would be dishonest to pretend that a chapter on the subject of staff development and inservice training could hope to stand austerely apart from the many recipes for effective teaching that are part and parcel of the initial and continuing education of teachers. However, the specific aims of the chapter are as follows:

1. To raise the question of teachers' rights and what have been called the 'special needs of teachers' (Galloway, 1985) within the context of meeting children's needs.
2. To describe some key recent and current developments in inservice education and to demonstrate how these utilise different models.

108

3. To examine how, within the perspectives of an ecological approach and collective responsibility (particularly as spelled out in Chapter 5), teachers can make self-appraisals of their existing skills and experiences and support each other in continued personal development.

How teachers can manage each other and themselves professionally is therefore one keynote of this chapter.

So emphasis will be placed on positively moving forward on the basis of current scenarios within primary schools rather than on easy invocation of 'teacher-deficit' models. A number of related conceptual issues will be touched upon, for this is an area that cannot lightly be represented by a set of prescriptions.

TEACHER TRAINING AND THE PLACE OF SPECIAL NEEDS

Since the concept of special needs has only been defined and officially used within the last ten years, it does not come as a surprise to discover that earlier textbooks for teachers in initial training do not mention the term. Post-Second World War teacher training might make mention of 'the slower learner' and touched upon remedial teaching; it may have made passing reference to mental and physical handicap. But, as the Warnock Report attested, hardly any training courses dealt properly with these elements.

However – and this may be one of the sources of the ambiguity identified and discussed below – attitudes to 'failing' children were, nevertheless, inculcated and shaped during initial teacher training by virtue of the curriculum components of the disciplines of sociology and psychology. Alexander (1984) has drawn attention to a subtle sensitising process that took place as students were introduced to concepts and evidence of inadequate family background, parental attitudes and their effects upon educational attainment. Schools were alleged to be able to 'compensate' for depriving circumstances only up to a point and certainly were absolved from even greater responsibility than that.

So a whole edifice was erected around confused and confusing aetiologies and 'cause and effect' theories. Educational psychologists have faced the dilemma for years as to whether or not to collude with the 'failing parents', 'inadequate home' explanation for educational underachievement and social maladjustment. Their own database has not been secure enough to effectively refute teachers' a priori judgements in this regard.

These remarks are less an indictment on a well-meaning profession than they are intended to sketch in some of the antecedents of the recent and current proliferation of inservice provision for special needs.

The Warnock Report expressed dissatisfaction with the piecemeal growth of specialisms within remedial and special education, which for many years came about pragmatically and 'on the job', rather than being linked to post-experience training. As far as delivering a unified service was concerned, the Report advocated the local creation of a Special Education Advisory and Support Service. Towards the medium- and longer-term ends of having such a unified service for special needs, which itself would be firmly embedded with integrated provision, the Report went on to consider how best initial and continuing training could develop over the next few years. The Committee's suggestions included a mandatory element in initial teacher training on special education and an available specialist special needs option. For inservice training they advocated short and longer local and accredited courses (pp. 355–7 of the Report for summary of recommendations).

Many initiatives of the last few years have flowed from these recommendations (see Croll and Moses, 1985, p. 153). What is important to note here is that the Warnock Report emphasised, if not the indivisibility between 'special' and 'ordinary', then the centrality of the concept of 'special' needs. The Report firmly places within the class teachers' orbit the responsibility for recognising 'early signs of possible special need . . . this requires that teachers should know how to identify the signs of special need' (p. 55, para. 4.18).

Textbooks written explicitly for intending teachers on special needs are sparse (see Sewell, 1986; also Cohen and Cohen, 1986). Even in an exposition on 'collaborative teacher education' (Exeter University, 1986) individual learning needs, the broadest context of 'special' needs, are not explored as a valid aspect of more recent forms of collaborative work between teacher training institutions and schools. Although the editor of the pamphlet affirms that the old demarcations of the four main educational disciplines have gone, he does not suggest what ideology of 'education for all' should inform a model of teacher training such as IT-INSET (see Preston, 1986; Ashton, 1986). However, Gulliford (1985) described encouraging signs that consideration of special needs was being incorporated into initial training.

PROFESSIONAL DEVELOPMENT AND SPECIAL NEEDS: SOME ISSUES

Contradictions

The nature of the word 'training' is discussed in some books cited in this section and, as we shall see, there is an array of inservice opportunities that encompass qualitative and practical aspects. In the prescriptions and training models that have emanated from the various bodies cited at the outset of the chapter, one can discern an ambiguity. On the one hand, as Warnock says, teachers trained to teach ordinary classes should be equipped to recognise and cope with special needs; on the other hand, special needs are seen as a responsibility for specialists. It is indeed a thin dividing line – the balancing act for LEAs has been to ensure adequate inservice training for special needs for 'ordinary' teachers whilst at the same time guaranteeing support to them from specialists, who also have a training agenda. One part of this dilemma is exposed by Sayer (1985), who asks:

> Do we want in any one school or group of schools a distinct body of specific professionals whose sole activity is to be a specialist resource to others or to children with special needs and who therefore lose much of their initial training as 'ordinary' teachers? (p. 3)

Whose responsibility is it to address the central issue; are the skills and expertise seen to be needed for special needs teaching different from core teaching skills for teaching all children? The question is rhetorical as far as this book is concerned, since it is too vast in scope to be resolved within one chapter. Another inherent issue within special needs inservice is the possible danger of 'deskilling teachers' and leading them 'to believe that only specialists can help children with special needs and that their own pedagogic skills are irrelevant' (Mongon, 1985, p. 45). So how can teachers best be assisted to feel confident that 'there is no mystique about remedial education nor are its methods intrinsically different from those employed by successful teachers anywhere'? (Gulliford, 1985, p. 22, quoting from the Bullock Report.) All that 'successful teachers' have to do, it seems, is to apply 'good teaching in such a way that failure is replaced by a sense of achievement' (Gulliford, op. cit.).

To what extent does the National Curriculum and the bedrock principle of entitlement of access of all children to all curriculum opportunities actually reinforce Gulliford's stance? Or is there a double message at the heart of the ERA/special needs debate that reinforces the contradiction, namely that 'special needs' should not be so diffused into the mainstream as to (a) deny some children their own distinctive or 'special' needs; (b) blunt teachers' sensitivity towards recognising, identifying, dealing with special needs? The premise in this section is that if children are seen to have rights, these can be expressed and realised if their teachers' rights are also acknowledged.

Invoking what they regard as appropriate language, some writers have expressed these rights in terms of 'teachers' special needs'. Gipps and Gross (1985) concluded from their survey:

what this does show is that unless teachers are involved in the developments, feel consulted and communicated with, they will feel dissatisfied
and disaffected; teachers do have special needs too. (p. 28)

Galloway (1985) devoted a chapter to the 'special educational needs of
teachers' and reviewed the notions of stress and satisfaction in teaching
with particular reference to special needs. He is of the opinion that it is
a 'neglected aspect of special educational needs, namely the effect of the
school's climate on its teachers as well as on its pupils' (p. 158). The
budding literature on teacher stress in the United Kingdom is one mani-
festation of the growing view that teachers have the right to have their
own professional needs met (ESAC, 1990).

Maybe one requisite of local inservice ought to be an exercise early
during a course on self and group identification of what participants
perceive their training needs to be, within the aims and objectives of the
particular course. This activity could generate further identification of
their rights *vis-à-vis* the broader context of their LEA policy and provision for special needs.

Teaching qualities

It is a bold person who attempts to define what a 'good' teacher is
and braves accusations of 'value judgements'. Haysom (1986) reflects,
after years spent in education, that 'the qualities or characteristics
of good teaching cannot be defined' (p. 30). Yet the DES has the temer-
ity to do just that (1985). In a paragraph entitled 'qualities of good
teachers' the reader is treated to a number of characteristics that make
up the good teacher. These are reminiscent of pulpit-thumping
sermons to 'be reliable, punctual, co-operative', 'willing to take on
essential tasks which relate to the care and safety of those in their
charge', 'they are of such a personality and character that they are able
to command the respect of their pupils', 'their genuine interest and
curiosity about what pupils say and think and the quality of their
professional concern for individuals' (pp. 2 and 3). The DES sees fit to
list the ingredients for the meal but leaves the making and consumption
to others.

The attributes of good teaching have clear implications for all teachers, who presumably hold an ideal picture and aspire to act like that
ideal, even if in reality they do not. But we might be on dangerous
ground if we thought it worth pursuing what the teaching qualities
should be of 'special needs' teachers as distinct from mainstream teachers. Surveys are reported by Wood (1984) into teachers' attitudes in the
United States regarding desirable attributes for mainstream and special
educators. The checklists thus generated reveal, perhaps unsur-
prisingly, few differences. Wood cites Crisci, who identifies nine major

categories of skills for both regular and special educations. These are: (1) assessment; (2) diagnosis; (3) prescription; (4) analysis; (5) behaviour management; (6) motivation; (7) communication; (8) evaluation; (9) human relations. They seem to be a mixture of nebulous 'fuzzy' qualities and more easily categorisable sets of specific skills.

Research into teaching qualities and requisite teaching skills continues (Kyriacou, 1990) and a new teacher-training project at Exeter University is attempting both to define the skills all competent teachers in primary education need and to encourage students to take a more analytical approach to their own teaching. The co-directors, Dunne and Harvard, have devised a nine-dimensional set of criteria: ethos; direct instruction; management of materials; guided practice; structured conversation; monitoring; management of order; planning and preparation; written evaluation. The advantages of this conceptually more rigorous approach over an approach like Crisci's is that all the identified aspects of teaching skill can be observed and evaluated by teachers themselves and other assessors.

THE SCOPE OF SPECIAL NEEDS INSERVICE TRAINING

Adams (1986) criticised the status quo at that time in these words:

> many (teachers) are ill-equipped to ensure that such needs are met. Some may have teaching qualifications but no specialist training for special needs; others may have specialist training but have not worked with pupils across the full ability range. The patterns of training must now be organised so as to prepare teachers more fully for their role in respect of pupils with special educational needs. (p. 124)

He went on to specify a number of possible ways in which local and regional inservice could be organised and set out explicitly the responsibilities in this regard of the LEA, HMI, and the DES and training institutions. These responsibilities devolve directly back onto schools: 'the head teacher of every school needs to be able to assume a full responsibility for ensuring that special educational needs are met' (p. 126).

During the 1980s there was a significant increase in special educational needs inservice training, which followed a number of patterns of delivery (see Table 6.1). In the last five or six years, the funding arrangements have changed several times; designated special educational needs categories have appeared in different DES circulars (GRIST, then LEATGS, then GEST, also ESG), thus earmarking and safeguarding moneys specifically for the purpose. One of the most

Table 6.1 *The pattern and scope of special needs inservice*

Content	Introduction to special needs for class teachers and/or newly-appointed special needs posts, covering:
	(i) awareness raising $\left.\begin{array}{l}\\\\\end{array}\right\}$ on special and remedial education, provision, curriculum approaches, work of support services
	(ii) developing knowledge-base
	Specific focus – finding out more about, for example, curriculum planning, school-based provision, language programmes, handicapping conditions and teaching implications
	'How to', for example, design and implement curricula, develop referral and liaison mechanisms, carry out classroom observation
	Conceptual and legislative issues, concept of special needs, integration, Education Act 1981, its procedures and ramifications
	Skills training in techniques directed towards competence in, for example, assessment, behaviourally based learning programmes, counselling
	Refresher update on any of the issues, techniques
Mode and timing	Full-time attendance, for example, one year, one term; part-time attendance; for example, day release, evening (after-school); series of workshops, for example, weekly; one-day course/conference; one session
Location	University, polytechnic, college; LEA centre; individual school

significant developments has been what were initially called 'Baker days' (after the then Secretary of State for Education). The Baker-day model represented a departure from established arrangements and LEA control to a situation where schools were given specific inservice training funds and a number of designated training days. So schools could, and do, set their own training agenda for in-house activities based on their own analyses of need, and of course LMS is a logical sequitur to this arrangement. Sebba and Robson (1988) describe school-focused INSET courses on special educational needs, give their evaluation of this initiative and provide an evaluation checklist (also see Lavers, Pickup and Thomson, 1989).

INITIATIVES IN INSERVICE TRAINING FOR SPECIAL NEEDS

School-focused INSET as a burgeoning area was mentioned above to demonstrate the broadened scope of inservice provision (and see Easen, 1985 and Hewton, 1988 for guidance on developing school-focused staff development). There are many initiatives encompassing the spectrum presented in Table 6.1. A brief résumé of some of them follows, with references where available. These initiatives are representative of countless such ventures.

Courses based in academic institutions with accreditation

Distance learning (with local tutorial support)

The seminal and unique course is the 'Special Needs in Education' course (E241) at the Open University. Booth (1985) described the genesis and the thinking behind the course, which produced over a dozen course books as well as several major free-standing texts, some of which have been referred to in this book since they are invaluable source books for debate and future planning. From 1991 E241 is replaced by E242, 'Learning for All'. Another new course is Advanced Diploma E806, Applied Studies in Learning Difficulties.

Full-time or part-time modes

These are courses that lead to a Diploma or Advanced Diploma, or Master's Degree (see Wedell, 1985). One of the prime aims of such courses is to provide special needs resource/advisory teachers, mostly to be deployed in schools. The Institute of Education, London University, offers a full-time Diploma in the Psychology of Education of Children with Special Needs, and also offers this course at Master's (MSc) level.

Norwich and Cowne (1985) describe the innovative one-term course in special needs at the Institute of Education, London University. It serves the London and Home Counties region, and is project-based and school-focused. Each participant, in co-operation with school colleagues, LEA staff and academic personnel, plans an intervention which will take place over a specified time. The emphasis is on context-bound problem definition, analysis and solution. 'Through the course members project the aim to help each school recognise its responsibilities for the special needs of its pupils' (Norwich and Cowne, p. 169; see also Newton and Hill (1985) for a description of a one-term course).

Courses, conferences run by professional and voluntary associations

Professional associations that run courses include the National Association for Remedial Education (NARE) and the National Council for Special Education (NCSE).[1] Amongst voluntary organisations that run national, regional and local meetings, sometimes tailor-made (i.e. responding to local need, or a local request), are the Down's Association, MENCAP, the Centre for Studies on Integration in Education, and the Spastics Society, which has run training programmes for years at its Castle Priory centre in Wallingford, Berkshire.

Local, national courses on particular technologies (skills-based) and training packages

In recent years as coherent 'packages' (blending theory and practice) have been developed, so training in these mostly behaviourally based programmes has been made available through local and regional networks. These include approaches that have been described elsewhere in this book, such as: EDY (Chapter 6), DATAPAC (Chapter 3), PORTAGE (Chapters 3 and 5), BATPACK (Chapter 4). Staff on these courses may be the original developers or locally trained personnel. Other examples of such packages include PATHFINDER from Surrey LEA (now PATHWAY: see Halliwell and Williams, 1991), which sets out sequential and multi-layered procedures for identifying, referring and intervening with special needs, and TIPS (1985).

LEA-instigated inservice

A considerable amount of LEA inservice on special needs was of course generated by the advent of the 1981 Education Act and every LEA runs some forms of INSET.

Bryans and Levey, in an area of Birmingham, initiated one such course for primary schools. Levey and Mallon (1984) describe the first and subsequent courses for which the broad aims were to:

- disseminate information and skills developed from psychology to as many primary caregivers as possible
- provide advice about individual problems with the minimum of delay.

Typical aims and objectives for LEA-initiated courses include to:

- consider procedures in schools for the identification of pupils with special needs
- help to provide an appropriate curriculum for these pupils
- enable early exchange of information between schools (both mainstream and special), support services and administration.

Hinson (1990) describes a rolling programme aimed at headteachers and designated special needs teachers and points to the fact that with staff turnover there is a continuing need for such a programme.

Whole-LEA approach

There are at present only a small number of LEAs that have a co-ordinated approach to special needs policy, as reflected in a comprehensive, systematically planned inservice programme. The Coventry
Special Needs Action Programme (SNAP), first described in Chapter
3, is the best developed to date with a wealth of handbooks, checklists,
video materials, and an extensive school-focused inservice programme. This can be targeted to individual schools, with continuing
support directed to those schools. In principle, as well as in practice,
the whole programme is a demonstration of collective responsibility.
As with PORTAGE, the organisational and managerial components
of SNAP are paramount, and SNAP utilises a pyramid model (Muncey
and Ainscow, 1983). Muncey (1986) lists the features of SNAP thus:

- early identification
- involvement of all teachers
- practical content
- active learning
- competency-based
- multimedia modules
- tutored by practising teachers
- staff support
- course development and dissemination.

It was mentioned in the previous chapter that the impetus for joint
multidisciplinary and inter-service awareness-raising and information exchange has been the 1981 Education Act. To a lesser extent the
1988 Education Reform Act has continued and will continue to
generate some shared initiatives and the 1989 Children Act certainly
has and will. At national level the National Children's Bureau has
pioneered many day courses and conferences to bring together practitioners and managers from many different statutory and voluntary
services, and training packages to support these endeavours or inspire
others include TECMEDIA (1989), a joint enterprise from NCB,
London University Institute of Education and Oxford Polytechnic, and
the three packs published by NFER-Nelson with the umbrella title 'Professional Learning Resources' (NFER-Nelson, 1989).

PROSPECTS FOR SPECIAL NEEDS INSERVICE TRAINING

The ACSET report recommended the inclusion of special needs within
initial teacher training (see Sayer and Jones (1985) and their contributors

for close examination and discussion of the ACSET proposals). The government (DES) has in recent years signalled a clear commitment by including the area of special needs as one of the national priority areas for DES/LEA joint-funded (though in different proportions) inservice training.

The HMI report *Special Needs Issues* (1990) gives an overview of recent developments in provision in initial teacher training, pointing out the significantly increased special educational needs content but also the variable quality within and across providing institutions. It recommends a blend of three approaches: introductory elements; permeation; specialised options. The report likewise provides a brief review of inservice training, highlighting the need for developing expertise in the area of the National Curriculum and special needs and recommending the increased development and take-up of open learning materials. Upton *et al.* (1991) describe a whole range of inservice approaches.

Methods and materials have undoubtedly taken root but a number of overarching issues remain unresolved, such as that of the 'special expertise' identified at the start of the chapter and discussed by Bines (1989). How separate should special needs training be? How tenable is a 'special professionalism'? To what extent should special needs training be pragmatic (that is, enabling and supporting teachers to meet the pedagogical/curricular/pastoral needs of pupils in their charge) and/or reflective (encouraging intending and practising teachers to challenge their existing attitudes and practice)? According to Bines, a reflective approach would ensure that special needs are considered within the context of rights and opportunities.

TOWARDS A PROGRAMME OF STAFF DEVELOPMENT AND SUPPORT WITHIN SCHOOLS

Within the spirit of collective responsibility espoused in this book there is potential for considerable mutual support by staff encouraging each other to foster awareness, pursue knowledge, acquire skills.

It would be part and parcel of a school policy on special needs (Chapter 7) to include staff development; key roles could be ascribed to different members of staff, so that, instead of one member of staff being the recipient of inservice training, taking place elsewhere, various staff are involved in a number of parallel, shared initiatives.

Here are some suggestions:

- preparing and discussing 'case studies' of children in school; using these as exemplars for the evolution of classroom practice, curriculum innovation, how to meet the specific needs of children with sensory or physical disabilities

- setting up a small task force to consider how best to proceed towards functional integration
- staff taking on an assignment to 'job-swap' with special school staff as part of developing working links
- setting up a staff forum for the exchange of ideas and concerns over pertinent professional issues, including résumés of relevant research, thought-provoking articles and books. The forum could invite personnel from other services from time to time. From this 'interface' could flow a number of initiatives such as those suggested by Hanko (1985), which could be seen as part of school-based inservice provision.

Some of these ideas are already operating on a small scale within schools (Hodgson, Clunies-Ross and Hegarty, 1984). What is advocated here is the creation of a coherent school policy to support these ventures and ensure their viability. The introduction of school-based training days should increase the likelihood of some of these ideas coming to fruition. Hewton (1988) contains stimulus material.

APPRAISING TEACHING SKILLS

Appraisal of teacher competence and performance has been the subject of much debate in the teaching unions, and between the unions, the government and DES. Whatever formal arrangements are worked out and accepted in the long run, within the realm of meeting children's learning, and other, needs in primary schools, there is much that can be done by teachers themselves.

Too often teachers have been demoralised by constant exhortations and by charges that they do not possess the requisite skills and attributes (Adams, 1986). The best place from which to start any kind of self and collective appraisal and skills analysis is 'where one is now', asking 'What can we offer at present?', 'What skills do we currently have?'

There is no dearth of texts describing appraisal schemes, offering practical strategies (Bunnell, 1990; Wragg, 1990; Poster and Poster, 1991) and raising the many issues associated with appraisal of competence in the workplace, one of which is how to strike the necessary balance between an imposed structure and activities generated by the practitioners themselves. On the premise that such self-initiated and self-directed actions are the most effective starting point Moyles (1988) offers a practical guide to self-evaluation and Montgomery and Hadfield (1989) advocate an approach to appraisal that is firmly rooted in interaction with pupils.

Table 6.2 gives a suggested sequential model for individual and group appraisal that reinforces the idea that appraisal is a continuing and integral part of teaching.

The suggested exercises are intentionally presented in a sparse, abbreviated fashion in order to suggest but not to prescribe. In practice they would be demanding and complex, but worth doing to:

- effect a match between requirements of the job or role and the skills and expertise of the 'doer', and
- promote the confidence of any member of staff who is undertaking a new post or taking on an area of responsibility.

I have been involved in a number of such training and skills development activities with different groups, comprising teachers, parents and a variety of other professionals who work with children and parents. We have agreed that the initial brainstorming and conceptualisation that form stages 1 and 2 (Table 6.2) are not easy. For example, it turns out not to be a straightforward exercise to attempt to categorise one's experience as distinct from specific skills. However, the consensus has generally been that these are worthwhile first steps towards skills analysis, the identification of emerging skills considered necessary to do a particular job, and the training needs for doing that job 'properly' or fulfilling the role.

Braun and Lasher (1978) devoted a section of their book to 'role definition' and sought to guide teachers through an appraisal of their role *vis-à-vis* special needs children as well as to reassure them that current competence is the best springboard from which to proceed to take on different aspects of the job.

Mongon (1985) firmly put all special needs inservice provision for teachers into context when he wrote, 'it should be possible and more profitable to allow teachers to share and contextualise their experiences so they develop a theoretical perspective which illuminates and enhances their own work' (p. 44).

Table 6.2

Stages	Appraisal (self/group)	Phases	Carrying out the job/fulfilling the role
1	Analysis of current competence (experience and skills)	1	Define job or role
2	Identify further training and support needed to do job/role	2	Requirements of job or role
3	Record and monitor progress	3	Carry out job or role
4	Re-appraise skills and competence	4	Review job or role

This brings us back full circle to the start of this chapter, when the immense responsibility of the teacher towards meeting all needs was acknowledged. The goal of inservice support has to be the devising and execution of the best possible means to enable teachers to exercise their responsibilities confidently, to their own professional satisfaction, and as far as possible within their own control (Powell and Solity, 1990).

NOTE

1 NARE and NCSE have now (1992) combined to form NASEN, the National Association for Special Educational Needs.

REFERENCES

Adams, F. (ed.) (1986) *Special Education*. Harlow: Longman/Society of Education Officers.

Alexander, R. (1984) *Primary Teaching*. London: Holt, Rinehart & Winston.

Ashton, P. (1986) 'IT-INSET, its principles and practice'. In Exeter University, op. cit.

Bines, H. (1989) 'Developing a special professionalism: perspectives and practices in teacher training'. In Roaf, C. and Bines, H. (eds) *Needs, Rights and Opportunities*, ch. 10. Brighton: Falmer Press.

Booth, A. (1985) 'In-service training at the O.U.'. In Sayer and Jones, op. cit.

Braun, S. and Lasher, M. (1978) *Are You Ready to Mainstream?* Columbus, OH: Charles E. Merrill.

Bunnell, S. (1990) *Teacher Appraisal in Practice*. Oxford: Heinemann Education.

Cohen, A. and Cohen, L. (eds) (1986) *Special Educational Needs in the Ordinary School: A Sourcebook for Teachers*. London: Harper & Row.

Croll, P. and Moses, D. (1985) *One in Five: The Assessment and Incidence of Special Educational Needs*. London: Routledge & Kegan Paul.

DES (1985) *Education Observed 3: Good Teachers*. A paper by HM Inspectorate. London: HMSO.

Easen, P. (1985) *Making School-centred INSET Work*. Open University/ Croom Helm.

ESAC (Education Service Advisory Committee) (1990) *Managing Occupational Stress: A Guide for Managers and Teachers in the Schools Sector*. London: HMSO.

Exeter University (1986) *Collaborative Teacher Education*, Perspectives 25. Exeter: Exeter University School of Education.

Galloway, D. (1985) *Schools, Pupils and Special Educational Needs*. Beckenham: Croom Helm.

Gipps, C. and Gross, H. (1985) 'Do teachers have special needs too?' *Screening and Special Educational Needs in Schools Project*, Occasional Paper No. 5. London: University of London, Institute of Education.

Gulliford, R. (1985) 'The teacher's own resources'. In Smith, C. (ed.) *New Directions in Remedial Education*. Brighton: Falmer Press.

Halliwell, M. and Williams, T. (1991) *PATHWAY*. Windsor: NFER-Nelson.

Hanko, G. (1985) *Special Needs in Ordinary Classrooms*. Oxford: Basil Blackwell.

Haysom, J. (1986) 'Teacher education: the relation between theory and practice'. In Exeter University, op. cit.

Hewton, E. (1988) *School-focused Staff Development*. Lewes: Falmer Press.

Hinson, M. (1990) Awareness of special needs in primary schools. *Support for Learning* 5 (1) (February), 22–30.

HMI (1990) *Special Needs Issues: A Survey by HMI*. London: HMSO.

Hodgson, A., Clunies-Ross, L. and Hegarty, S. (1984) *Learning Together: Teaching Pupils with Special Educational Needs in the Ordinary School*. Windsor: NFER-Nelson.

Kyriacou, C. (1990) *Essential Teaching Skills*. Oxford: Blackwell.

Lavers, C., Pickup, M. and Thomson, M. (1989) SEN: A school-based INSET package. *Support for Learning* 4 (2) (May), 90–96.

Levey, M. and Mallon, F. (1984) Support and advisory groups in primary schools. *Journal of the Association of Educational Psychologists* 6 (4) (Summer).

Mongon, D. (1985) 'Patterns of delivery and implications for training'. In Sayer and Jones, op. cit.

Montgomery, D. and Hadfield, N. (1989) *Appraisal in Primary Schools*. Leamington Spa: Scholastic Publications.

Moyles, J. (1988) *Self-evaluation: A Primary Teachers' Guide*. Windsor: NFER-Nelson.

Muncey, J. (1986) 'Meeting special needs in mainstream schools'. Coventry Education Department.

Muncey, J. and Ainscow, M. (1983) Launching SNAP in Coventry. *British Journal of Special Education* 10 (3) (September).

Newton, M. and Hill, D. (1985) Special educational needs in the ordinary school: a new initiative. *Remedial Education* 20 (4) (November).

NFER-Nelson (1988) *Professional Learning Resources*: Douglas, J. (ed.) *Emotional and Behavioral Problems in Young Children*; Monck, E. (ed.) *Emotional and Behavioral Problems in Adolescence*; Smith, J. and Bryans, J. (eds) *Issues on Statementing Children with Emotional and Behavioral Problems*.

Norwich, B. and Cowne, E. (1985) Training with a school focus. *British Journal of Special Education* 12 (4) (December).

Poster, C. and Poster, D. (1991) *Teacher Appraisal: A Guide to Training*. London: Routledge.

Powell, M. and Solity, J. (1990) *Teachers in Control: Cracking the Code*. London: Routledge.

Preston, M. (1986) 'IT-INSET at Widey Court?' In Exeter University, op. cit.

Pumfrey, P. (1991) *Improving Children's Reading in the Junior School: Challenges and Responses*. London: Cassell.

Sayer, J. (1985) 'Training for diversity: the context for change'. In Sayer and Jones, op. cit.

Sayer, J. and Jones, N. (eds) (1985) *Teacher Training and Special Educational Needs*. Beckenham: Croom Helm.

Sebba, J. (1985) The development and evaluation of short school-focused courses on special educational needs, *Educational and Child Psychology* 2 (3).

Sebba, J. and Robson, C. (1988) Evaluating short, school-focused INSET courses in special educational needs. *British Journal of Special Education* 15 (3) (Research supplement, September), 111–15.

Sewell, G. (1986) *Coping with Special Needs, A Guide for New Teachers.* Beckenham: Croom Helm.

TECMEDIA (1989) *Decision-making for Special Educational Needs: An Interservice Resource Pack.* TECMEDIA, 5 Granby Street, Loughborough LE11 3DU.

TIPS (Teacher Information Pack) (1985). Basingstoke: Macmillan.

Upton, G. *et al.* (1991) *Staff Training and Special Educational Needs.* London: David Fulton.

Wedell, K. (1985) 'Post-experience training'. In Sayer and Jones, op. cit.

Wood, J. (1984) *Adapting Instruction for the Mainstream.* Columbus, OH: Charles E. Merrill.

Wragg, E. (1990) *Teacher Appraisal: A Practical Guide.* London: Macmillan.

—7—

Determinants of policy and practice in the primary school

This penultimate chapter forms a summary, at the end of which the reader, having taken stock, may feel ready to pursue the theme of the final chapter, which is about transition and looking beyond the primary perimeters.

It also addresses some of the core components that could form an articulated policy for meeting children's needs in primary schools. Throughout the book there has been an intentional blurring of the concept of designated 'special' needs, a concept that serves a double-bind purpose: a statement of a child's special needs protects that child, whilst at the same time perpetuating his or her separateness from the mainstream.

How do 'ordinary' primary schools committed to comprehensive education for all come to terms with having to demarcate between ordinary and 'special' provision? How such schools are enabled to work towards a viable educational practice that can encompass all the children within their portals without stigma and without creating either élites or ghettos is the major and enduring educational challenge.

Primary education has rested for a long time on much collective received wisdom (to which the Plowden Report gave expression) about the criteria that constitute 'good' primary practice (Mittler, 1985). Whilst many of these guidelines may be proven precepts passed from one generation of teachers to the next, educationalists must now apply more stringent criteria that are empirically based rather than couched in fuzzy, exhortatory terms (cf. DES, 1985).

It is hopefully not too pious to say that we owe it to the children in schools to ensure that the ways in which classrooms are organised, curricula are planned, teaching staff are deployed and a caring climate is fostered are the result of in-depth investigation. We can begin, too, to take advantage of the increase in the range of educational research tools at our disposal – from the use of classical hypothesis-testing studies to the deployment of qualitative and ethnographic approaches (Hegarty and Evans, 1985). We still need to heed the proposals in the

Warnock Report for research into key areas at local and national levels (para. 18, 15, p. 322), although as LEAs fragment the opportunities for planned studies of this nature become less likely.

The rest of this chapter will be devoted to realistic possibilities for school-focused policy setting in a number of key areas, within delineated broad contexts.

DETERMINING SCHOOL POLICY ON SPECIAL NEEDS

The areas that will now be examined are perceived to be key components but are not all-inclusive. Thus this chapter is a guideline not a prescription.

Some of these components provide the common underpinning for specific areas that have been examined in previous chapters. It is suggested, as a basis for action, that each of these areas be considered by staff with a view to their inclusion in the school policy. These are:

- Home–school links and parental participation (Chapter 2)
- Management of learning (Chapter 3)
- Behaviour management (Chapter 4)
- Organisation of school, classroom and curriculum (Chapter 5)
- Staff development and support (Chapter 6)
- Liaison with support services (touched on in each of these chapters).

Each chapter has attempted to identify, even at points to spell out, what the policy-practice formula could be. Readers will recall that there has been a recurring plea for collective responsibility. Prefatory remarks at the outset of a policy statement could affirm a commitment to collective responsibility before defining what it means and how it would work in practice.

Figure 7.1, in diagram form, suggests a model for a policy statement. It would be for each school to flesh out, as precisely and concretely as is necessary, in the given situation, how the underpinning common components (no. 3 in the diagram) relate to each major element (no. 2). The relationship between the school and the LEA is demonstrated, and it is implicit that for every identified major element and common component unique to each school, the LEA as presently organised has a corresponding responsibility.

KEY STAFF

Within collective responsibility, staff members will have designated areas for which they are responsible and accountable. Some aspects of

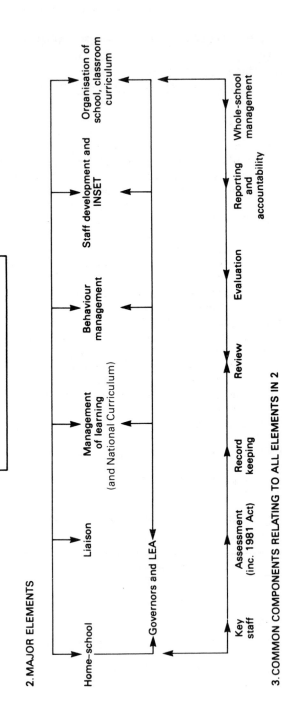

Figure 7.1 A primary school's policy statement on special needs: a suggested model

this were touched on in the previous chapter and, in particular, what some may see to be the central role of the special needs co-ordinator. However, what is specifically meant by 'key' staff members may not be synonymous with the overall brief to the co-ordinators' role.

What is proposed here is that any child deemed at any time to have special needs – a planned programme, access to certain resources – will have one key member of staff, or key worker, allocated to him or her, who will act as prime reference point, main liaison, and who may, too, accept responsibility for the execution of curriculum and other arrangements. In other words, the key staff member undertakes to 'manage' the special needs programme for that child and to initiate reviews. There is considerable local case study evidence that the absence of key workers can increase the risk of children slipping through various networks.

Certainly the key worker can also be the special needs co-ordinator. On the other hand, the decision as to who is best placed to act as key worker for a particular child will need to take account of that child's unique and current circumstances. So the class teacher may be best placed, or an attached or visiting teacher, the headteacher, or deputy; perhaps an education welfare officer or educational psychologist would be the most suitable person.

The four case study vignettes below illustrate, hypothetically, the assignment of a key worker who appears to be best placed to take on that role in the circumstances. The vignettes also make the point that we do now have a phalanx of highly qualified support staff who should not be regarded as peripheral to schools but who are integrally part of the collective response to children's needs. Each vignette sketches with minimum detail the provision each child currently receives, lists the people involved and briefly explains the logic and rationale behind the choice of key worker in each case.

Case study vignettes illustrating choice of key worker

No. 1 Colin aged 9 years; *hearing-impaired*
Provision: *in unit for hearing-impaired attached to junior school*
Personnel currently involved:
Class teacher
Visiting advisory teacher for hearing-impaired children (key worker)
Speech therapist at clinic
Teacher with responsibility for language development in the school
Educational psychologist
Parents

Choice of key worker:
The visiting advisory teacher is well placed by virtue of her speciality and expertise, her links with the other services and the school; and the fact that she has worked for two years with Colin and his parents, giving advice and support.

No. 2 Fiona aged 10 years*; in receipt of a Statement under the Education Act 1981, with 'moderate learning difficulties'*
Provision: *in junior school, in ordinary class, with curriculum support*
Personnel currently involved:
Class teacher
Special Needs Co-ordinator (key worker)
Visiting advisory teacher from local special school for moderate learning difficulties
Educational psychologist
Parents
Choice of key worker:
The Special Needs Co-ordinator is well placed, for she works closely with the class teacher and visiting teacher and has visited the latter's school. She has also worked towards involving Fiona's parents in school and home-based programmes. Her home visiting brief is an asset in this situation.

No. 3 Meryl aged 7 years*; with Down's syndrome*
Provision: *in top infants' class, in a school on the same campus as the junior school. She has 10 hours a week in school from the home liaison teacher. Reassessment of her needs is taking place.*
Personnel currently involved:
Class teacher (key worker)
Welfare assistant
Peripatetic home liaison teacher
Social worker for mental handicap
Educational psychologist
Parents
Choice of key worker:
In this instance, the class teacher was regarded as being centrally placed, working well with the home liaison teacher and developing a good relationship with Meryl and her parents. She would be the link between infant and junior, should a recommendation for continued integration be made.

No. 4 Rashid aged 8 years*; with physical handicap (spasticity)*
Provision: *in a special school for children with physical handicap and attending local junior school five mornings*

Personnel currently involved:
Class teacher of special school
Class teacher in junior school
Outreach teacher attached to junior school (with responsibility for home–school liaison for ethnic minorities)
Physiotherapist at clinic
Clinical Medical Officer, visits special school
Educational psychologist, visits both schools (key worker)
Parents
Choice of key worker:
It is part of Rashid's Statement of Needs that he should be in receipt of some integrated provision, towards the longer-term goal of going to the Secondary Unit for physically handicapped pupils on the same site as a comprehensive school. The educational psychologist is seen to have the best links with the unit, school, other services, and parents, and will be involved in the reassessment prior to secondary transfer. His involvement for the past three years and his overall knowledge of the situation make him well placed to be the key worker.

There are a number of issues relating to role boundary, lines of communication, the extent of the responsibility that a key worker takes on, or is empowered by others to take on. How viable and feasible in practice the idea of a key worker would be has yet to be determined on a wide scale. Circular 22/89 (DES, 1989) endorses the idea of 'befriender', which has been promoted in other quarters. Such a role would include acting on behalf of the pupil and family, and there are obvious parallels between this concept and that of a key worker.

ASSESSMENT AND RECORD-KEEPING

Whatever policy on assessment for special needs is adopted will be part of the school's overall strategies for assessing and monitoring progress and performance, within the mandatory framework of the National Curriculum and requirement for reporting progress. What is of concern is that there should be seen to be a coherent plan in respect of

- continuing record-keeping on the progress of all children
- first-phase record-keeping of concerns over children's progress
- agreed means of data collection (assessment, measuring, observation) and sharing of information at this early stage of concern
- second-phase closer-focused assessment leading to intervention, further action, e.g. referral onwards

- agreed use of forms of record-keeping to monitor action, progress, outcomes of intervention, decision-making.

Readers will find echoes in this list of Warnock's stages of assessment, and, indeed, this is intentional. The Warnock Committee members would wish that there had been, in these intervening years, a faster take-up and implementation of their rational plan for assessment stages and record-keeping.

It remains an untested hypothesis as to whether or not there would be more, or indeed fewer, referrals for Section 5 assessment if all schools had a tight, functional programme of close monitoring of progress.

This book has attempted to set the scene for the development of assessment, monitoring, and record-keeping procedures in the key areas of management of learning (Chapter 3) and behaviour management (Chapter 4). In both of those chapters charts were provided for assessment and intervention strategies which show the possible input of the various people involved – teachers, parents, child, psychologist and others. References were given to help set up comprehensive systems that would include commensurate record-keeping forms.

The key suggestion, first made in Chapter 1, elaborated in Chapter 3 and picked up once more in Chapter 4, is the formulation of a Learning Profile for each child. The concept remains a cornerstone that combines assessment, monitoring of progress and record-keeping. It is deliberately not specified too much, except for the descriptive notes and illustrative case study provided in Appendix 1, so that practitioners might evolve their own version of either or both the Learning Profile and a complementary Behaviour Profile – or these could be one and the same as in the original conception, i.e. a composite Child Profile.

Involving parents in assessment

The parental contribution to assessment should now be integral to a school's assessment policy and can take various forms, for example:

- home-based observation and recording in diary or chart form (references in Chapters 3 and 4)
- completion of developmental, skills or behaviour checklists, rating scales
- constructing 'My Child at Home' parental profile. This author explored the potential of the parental profile extensively, and the subject was mentioned in Chapter 3. Appendix 2 provides Notes for Parents, which can be used by parents and practitioners as a guideline for the creation of a parental profile.

The rationale behind involving parents in assessment is that of 'equivalent expertise' (Wolfendale, 1983, 1988; see also Chapter 2, this book), that is, the pooling and sharing of information by people closely involved with and responsible for any one child. This complementary exercise yields rich information about the different aspects of a child's life and functioning, providing a more accurate database for all concerned (and see Appendix 5 for the eco-mapping exercises which are consistent with these developments). Appendix 4 contains as a flow-chart a sequential outline of joint involvement in assessment demonstrating parallel and related activities by parents and professionals. Now, with the requirement for schools to report on children's progress to parents, there is much potential in the idea of 'reciprocal reporting', elaborated in Wolfendale (1991), that is, school to home and vice versa.

Galloway's chapter on assessment (Galloway, 1985) is a useful distillation of the purposes, stages and mechanics of assessment. He welds his overview onto an appraisal of formal assessments and statementing under the 1981 Education Act, i.e. how these relate to school-based assessment. Much recent LEA inservice training on the Act has sought to demonstrate the relevance of the formal procedures to all schools, to show how the 'educational advice' provided by teachers ought to be based on really detailed prior notes, records and assessment of progress and problems as well as on the concurrent assessment required under the Act.

The message in this section is that a school's policy towards formal and other special needs assessment (and review) must be an integral part of a whole-school policy, particularly now when assessment arrangements are built into ERA (DES, 1989).

REVIEW, EVALUATION AND ACCOUNTABILITY

Review of schools' procedures and provision was referred to briefly in the previous chapter within the context of management. Abbott (1986) refers to school-based review and self-evaluation schemes as being nowadays accepted as 'one of the major strategies for achieving school improvement'. The development of school-based review procedures has, Abbott avers, helped schools to assume responsibility for their own effectiveness, in turn offering a basis for accountability 'which is honest and realistic' (p. 3). In his short summary article, Abbott drew on the GRIDS ('Guidelines for Review and Internal Development in Schools') project, which offers a number of basic principles, indeed requisites, for effective school-based review that can apply to primary, secondary and special school sectors.

Galvin (1987) offers a model whereby using GRIDS' format, provision for behaviour problems within schools can be appraised. Other topics that form part of the special needs area can be appraised by using the GRIDS' five stages, or any other process model. For example, ways in which the management of learning is organised within the school can be examined through a process that includes reviewing:

- curriculum arrangements for children with identified learning difficulties
- how children with disabilities are assisted and supported in class
- arrangements for inservice and staff development on learning difficulties, curriculum development, professional skills
- available and needed resources, materials, and aids to learning.

The GRIDS' five stages – getting started, initial review; specific review(s); action for development; overview and restart – can be applied as the conceptual framework for the exercise of reviewing the management of learning.

McMahon *et al.* (1984) point out that priority setting is one of the first tasks in determining which areas shall be reviewed. With reference to the suggested policy model shown diagrammatically in Figure 7.1, given that not all areas can be simultaneously reviewed, it is suggested here that areas for review can be prioritised or rotated. Review and evaluation procedures are amongst the common underpinning components in the diagram.

It is consistent with the rapprochement between primary and special education traditions defined and delineated in Chapter 1 that in this chapter there should be a plea for primary educators to broaden principles and practice of evaluation to incorporate the hitherto quite separate and distinctive areas of 'special' and 'remedial'.

The slogan 'every teacher is a special needs teacher' is said to be most applicable at the primary stage where a small number of teachers are significant in each child's life. Yet this book has been at pains to demonstrate the insufficiency of invoking that slogan without the creation and maintenance of a whole back-up of LEA-supported and school-based developing expertise, professional confidence, well-considered curriculum, resource, staffing and liaison arrangements.

Evaluation of these practices would seem, nowadays, to be a mandatory part of education. The existence of recent legislative frameworks (e.g. the 1980, 1981, 1986 and 1988 Education Acts) have strong implications for the duties of LEAs, education committees and schools' governing bodies. Thomas (1985) points to the purposes of evaluating the many and varied educational activities and considers for whom evaluation is carried out. In a broad-based model of the interrelationship of evaluation and accountability, schools' central place within the locality as a community resource becomes clear. Parents need to see and participate in the opening up of educational processes and exercise their rights for access to information and to be consulted. The 1988 Education Reform Act purposefully promotes parental choice, participation and decision-making in a key number of education areas and processes.

One keyword for effective evaluation of educational processes and activities may well be consultation. Alexander remarks (1984) that teachers should participate in evaluation exercises or these become meaningless. Unless the analogy is extended in execution beyond the schools' confines to the broader reaches of parental and community participation, the value of 'checklist' or any other type of evaluation described by Alexander is reduced (Abbott, Birchenaugh and Steadman, 1989).

A useful compendium providing valuation frameworks, strategies, and methodology is that of Rodger and Richardson (1985). The five 'areas of concern' identified by Rodger and Richardson are perennial features of school life:

- school climate/ethos
- curriculum
- monitoring of pupil progress
- management of resources
- relationships with the community.

It would be compatible to make a match between those elements identified above in Figure 7.1 as comprising a primary school's policy on special needs with these five major enduring features. The successful design and execution of evaluation exercises on any one or more of these features could be a powerful demonstration of true integrated provision – that is, progress of individual children is appraised within the context of appraisal of whole-school processes. By these means the synthesis between primary and special education traditions is seen to be symbiotic and a force for positive change. Rodger and Richardson provide plenty of tasks and practical examples of evaluation exercises. Interestingly they suggest a brainstorming activity using a debating format on the issue of integrated versus segregated education (p. 179).

As has already been hinted at above, accountability runs as a thread through all review and evaluation approaches. Much has been written on the purposes of accountability and the procedures whereby educational practice is made accountable to children themselves, parents, governors, the LEA and Committees (Hughes, Ribbins and Thomas, 1985). The debate on accountability has been sharpened with the advent of ERA and its emphasis on market forces, consumer choice, quality assurance and the concomitant forms of public accountability that the new procedures have brought about. For example, there has been discussion on the viability of producing performance indicators for schools as one means by which schools are seen to deliver what they say they do (SIS, 1988; Fitz-Gibbon, 1990). Many parents would welcome inclusion of special needs policies into schools' review and accountability procedures.

WHOLE-SCHOOL MANAGEMENT

The final common component underpinning the major elements of a primary school's special needs policy (see Figure 7.1 above), that of 'whole-school management', has in essence been the substance of this volume. In keeping with the companion foundation book on special educational needs in secondary schools in this series, this book has emphasised throughout, in a number of ways, the importance of effective management – that is, the initiation and surveillance of change, the orchestration of all the planning, organisation, and execution of those initiatives.

In a book concerned with equalisation of opportunities to fully involve all children within the mainstream of education, devising and carrying out a policy on special needs in primary schools is to be regarded as an expression of human rights. An emphasis has been given to teachers', children's and parents' needs, amongst which are granting of rights that have then to be taken up. That schools and LEAs were beginning to take seriously their ethical as well as their pedagogic responsibility in respect of 'needs' was attested in DES (1986). LEA replies demonstrated a general commitment in the education service to the integration of special needs provision into the general structure of education.

A range of initiatives was mentioned:

- inservice training
- appointment of co-ordinators
- advisory teachers
- deployment of teachers with special education qualifications in ordinary schools
- production of special teaching materials.

A policy for meeting special educational needs in primary schools amounts to a Code of Practice for ensuring that children's learning and other needs can and will be met in schools, via a series of statements that reflect unanimity of purpose within a framework of collective responsibility.

From the ILEA's Junior School Project, twelve key factors of effectiveness were identified. These were:

1. Purposeful leadership of the staff by the head teacher.
2. The involvement of the deputy head.
3. The involvement of teachers.
4. Consistency amongst teachers.
5. Structured sessions.
6. Intellectually challenging teaching.
7. Work-centred environment.
8. Limited focus within sessions.
9. Maximum communication between teachers and pupils.
10. Record-keeping.
11. Parental involvement.
12. Positive climate.

The authors (Mortimore, 1989) say that, whilst these twelve factors do not constitute a 'recipe' for effective junior schooling, they can provide a framework within which the various partners in the life of the school can operate. They cite as the partners headteacher and staff, parents and pupils and governors. 'Each of these partners has the capacity to foster the success of the school. When each participant plays a positive role, the result is an effective school' (p. 38).

What will make for an effective school in the 1990s is considered by Reynolds (1991), and clearly there is an emphasis upon 'new management tasks' as well as upon the idea of planning for school development (Hargreaves, 1989). Such an audit reinforces the notion of collective responsibility.

WHOLE-SCHOOL POLICY ON SPECIAL EDUCATIONAL NEEDS

There is now no shortage of ideas, strategies and prescriptions for adopting a 'macro' approach to special needs. The ideology propagated by this and other writers is an equal opportunities one, in which special needs are identified as a distinctive, but not separate or marginalised, area. Some of the writers concentrate on a pragmatic approach, offering guidelines for action (Gordon, 1989). Others, like this author, identify components for whole-school policy (see also Wade and Moore, 1987; Bines, 1989). Thomas and Feiler (1988) epitomise the 'macro' approach by outlining a broader, ecological context to a whole-school special needs policy, and Dessent (1987) is largely issues-led, with an emphasis on the need for curriculum differentiation as a key plank of such a policy. The following two definitions of whole-school special needs policies are offered by Roaf (1988) and Ainscow and Florek (1990):

> A policy clearly understood by the whole school community whose purpose is to guide and determine the ethos of the school and to support attitudes and behaviour consistent with that ethos. (Roaf, 1988, p. 8)

> A whole school approach is where attempts are being made to utilise all the resources of a school to foster the development of all its children (Ainscow and Florek, 1990, p. 3)

An example of a practitioner-led process model is provided by current work by the Learning Support Service in the London Borough of Newham (Hardy and Hunt, 1991), in which team members wrote a draft document entitled *Whole-school Approaches to Assessment and Special Educational Needs*, put it out for consultation, and revised it. The plan is that it will be adopted by schools and will create a common framework for discussion and action.

THE BROADER CONTEXT TO COLLECTIVE RESPONSIBILITY

Although this book is about primary schools and for primary teachers, a recurrent theme has been liaison and communication within and outside school. Administrative personnel from the LEA, support services, governors, parents and pupils themselves are integral to the exercise of creating and maintaining special educational needs policies.

Figure 7.2 indicates these participants, and lists the substance and scope of their respective remit and responsibilities. The chart has been tried out and revised in a series of inservice exercises. One way of generating discussion and ideas is to present only the headings and ask participants to suggest what should go in each list. This encourages close identification of participants with the issues and reinforces the notion and principles of collective responsibility.

REFERENCES

Abbott, R. (1986) School-based review: plague or panacea? *School Curriculum Development Committee LINK* 4.

Abbott, R., Birchenaugh, M. and Steadman. S. (1989) *External Perspectives in School-Based Review*. York: Longman.

Ainscow, M. and Florek, A. (eds) (1990) *Special Educational Needs: Towards a Whole-school Approach*. London: Fulton.

Alexander, R. (1984) *Primary Teaching*. London: Holt, Rinehart & Winston.

Bines, H. (1989) Whole school policies at primary level. *British Journal of Special Education* 16 (2) (June), 80–82.

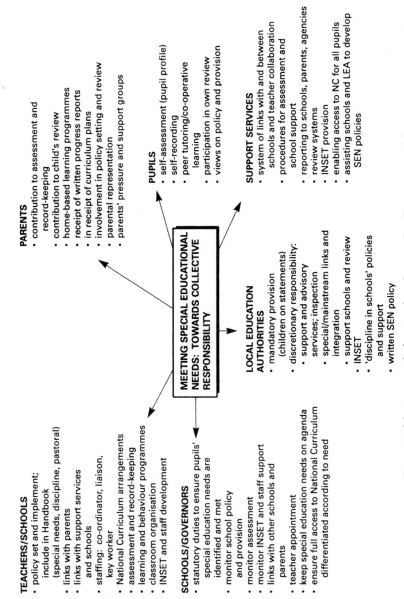

PARENTS
- contribution to assessment and record-keeping
- contribution to child's review
- home-based learning programmes
- receipt of written progress reports
- in receipt of curriculum plans
- involvement in policy setting and review
- parental representation
- parents' pressure and support groups

PUPILS
- self-assessment (pupil profile)
- self-recording
- peer tutoring/co-operative learning
- participation in own review
- views on policy and provision

SUPPORT SERVICES
- system of links with and between schools and teacher collaboration
- procedures for assessment and school support
- reporting to schools, parents, agencies
- review systems
- INSET provision
- enabling access to NC for all pupils
- assisting schools and LEA to develop SEN policies

MEETING SPECIAL EDUCATIONAL NEEDS: TOWARDS COLLECTIVE RESPONSIBILITY

LOCAL EDUCATION AUTHORITIES
- mandatory provision (children on statements)
- discretionary responsibility:
- support and advisory services; inspection
- special/mainstream links and integration
- support schools and review
- INSET
- 'discipline in schools' policies and support
- written SEN policy

TEACHERS/SCHOOLS
- policy set and implement; include in Handbook (special needs, discipline, pastoral)
- links with parents
- links with support services and schools
- staffing: co-ordinator, liaison, key worker
- National Curriculum arrangements
- assessment and record-keeping
- learning and behaviour programmes
- classroom organisation
- INSET and staff development

SCHOOLS/GOVERNORS
- statutory duties to ensure pupils' special education needs are identified and met
- monitor school policy and provision
- monitor assessment
- monitor INSET and staff support
- links with other schools and parents
- teacher appointment
- keep special education needs on agenda
- ensure full access to National Curriculum differentiated according to need

Figure 7.2 Meeting special educational needs: towards collective responsibility

DES (1985) *Education Observed 3: Good Teachers*. A paper by HMI Inspectorate. London: HMSO.

DES (1986) *Local Authority Policies for the School Curriculum*. Report on the Circular 8/83 Review. London: HMSO.

DES (1989) *Assessments and Statements of Special Educational Needs: Procedures within the Education, Health and Social Services*, Circular 22/89. London: DES.

Dessent, A. (1987) *Making the Ordinary School Special*. Lewes: Falmer Press.

Fitz-Gibbon, C. (ed.) (1990) *Performance Indicators*, BERA Dialogues no. 2. Clevedon: Multilingual Matters.

Galloway, D, (1985) *Schools, Pupils and Special Educational Needs*. Beckenham: Croom Helm.

Galvin, P. (1987) *Behaviour Management: Levels of Intervention*. Windsor: NFER-Nelson.

Gipps, C. and Gross, H. (1986) 'Children with special needs in primary school: where are we now?' British Educational Research Association Annual Conference, Institute of Education, London University.

Gipps, C., Steadman, S., Blackstone, T. and Stierer, B. (1983) *Testing Children: Standardised Testing in LEAs and Schools*. London: Heinemann.

Gordon, V. (1989) *Your Primary School: Your Policy for Special Eduational Needs*. Stafford: National Association for Remedial Education.

GRIDS (Guidelines for review and internal development in schools). School Curriculum Development Committee, Newcombe House, 45 Notting Hill Gate, London W11 3JB.

Hardy, C. and Hunt, J. (1991) *Whole-school Approaches to Assessment and Special Educational Needs*. London: Borough of Newham, Learning Support Service.

Hargreaves, D., Hopkins, D., Leask, M., Connolly, J. and Robinson, P. (1989) *Planning for School Development: Advice to Governors, Headteachers and Teachers*. London: DES/HMSO.

Hegarty, S. and Evans, P. (eds) (1985) *Research and Evaluation Methods in Special Education: Quantitative and Qualitative Techniques in Case Study Work*. Windsor: NFER-Nelson.

Hughes, M., Ribbins, P. and Thomas, H. (eds) (1985) *Managing Education: The System and the Institution*. Eastbourne: Holt, Rinehart & Winston.

McMahon, A., Bolam, R., Abbott, R. and Holly, P. (1984) *Guidelines for Review and Internal Development in Schools, A Primary Handbook*. York: Longman/Schools Council.

Mittler, P. (1985) 'Approaches to evaluation for special education: concluding reflections'. In Hegarty and Evans, op. cit.

Mortimore, P. (1989) 'School matters'. In Moon, B., Murphy, P. and Raynor, J. (eds) *Policies for the Curriculum*. London: Hodder & Stoughton/Open University.

Reynolds, D. (1991) School effectiveness and school improvement in the 1990s. *Newsletter of the Association for Child Psychology and Psychiatry* **13** (2), (March), 5–10.

Roaf, C. (1988) 'The concept of a whole-school approach to special need'. In Robinson, O. and Thomas, G. (eds) *Tackling Learning Difficulties*. Sevenoaks: Hodder & Stoughton.

Rodger, T.A. and Richardson, J.A.S. (1985) *Self-Evaluation for Primary Schools*. Sevenoaks : Hodder & Stoughton.

SIS (1988) *Performance Indicators for Schools: A Consultation Document*. Statistical Information Service, 3 Robert Street, London WC2 6BH.

Thomas, G. and Feiler, A. (eds) (1988) *Planning for Special Needs: A Whole-school Approach*. Oxford: Basil Blackwell.

Thomas, H. (1985) 'Perspectives on evaluation'. In Hughes *et al.*, op. cit.

Wade, B. and Moore, M. (1987) *Special Children – Special Needs: Provision in Ordinary Classrooms*. London: Robert Royce.

Wolfendale, S. (1983) *Parental Participation in Children's Development and Education*. London: Gordon & Breach.

Wolfendale, S. (1988) *The Parental Contribution to Assessment*. Developing Horizons no. 10. Stratford upon Avon: National Council for Special Education.

Wolfendale, S. (1991) 'Parents and teachers working together on the assessment of children's progress'. In Lindsay, G. and Miller, A. (eds) *Psychological Services for Primary Schools*. York: Longman.

Prospects: sharing responsibility for transfer to secondary school

Collective responsibility for special educational needs in primary school ends, in an executive sense, when children leave behind their primary schooldays to enter secondary school. But the influence of collective responsibility in action will reverberate into the secondary sector. If primary staff have done an effective job of co-ordination and liaison from entry to exit points, then their children stand a better chance of settling into their new milieu.

The adoption of the first/middle/high school model in many LEAs has reflected the unease over the traditional rigid demarcation between primary and secondary sectors and the massive differences in size, organisation and curriculum. The middle/high school debate properly belongs to an arena other than this book – suffice to say that the movement has constituted an attempt to bridge the artificial developmental divide of primary/secondary and to render more smooth the transition to other stages of education.

The primary/secondary demarcation, however, remains the norm, though few LEAs have had a clear-cut, articulated policy for effecting smooth transfer. Educationalists have not yet evolved viable models for handling transfer and for dealing with the personal, emotional and intellectual challenges each child has to face at this crucial stage.

Not surprisingly, therefore, the child with special needs is even more vulnerable at this critical time. The familiar and supportive struts of school are removed and the child has to face, with minimum support from new teachers, profound readjustment and realignment within an initially alien, even alienating, environment.

The moral responsibility inherent in implementing equal opportunities to ensure access to a broad range of experiences by all children must extend beyond the discrete enclaves of primary/secondary schools to guarantee that children's special needs are met at transfer time. Planned continuity has to be one of the cornerstones of integrated provision. For those children for whom the LEA maintains a statement of needs, as well as for other children, the provisions, resources, and staffing available in one setting must be equally available in the next.

This short final chapter addresses itself to some of the practical issues and mechanisms of transfer and raises questions for debate within schools about the broader longer-term areas of responsibility of primary school staff *vis-à-vis* preparing children to attain their life goals.

EFFECTING TRANSFER FROM AND CONTINUITY BETWEEN PRIMARY AND SECONDARY SCHOOLING

1. Guidelines for supporting transfer

There are some texts and studies in this relatively neglected area which serve as signposts. Youngman and Lunzer (1977) pointed out that there was little research in the area prior to their own study, the major British study having been that of Nisbet and Entwhistle (1969). Youngman and Lunzer set out to examine 'the transfer problem' and explored children's attitudes, motivation, anxieties and adjustment.

Later studies into transfer in these middle years, whether primary to secondary, middle to high schools, have been those of Galton and Willcocks (1984), which was part of the ORACLE study (referred to in Chapter 5), Taylor and Garson (1982), Measor and Woods (1984) and Stillman and Maychall (1984).

These studies have been concerned to produce guidelines for staff, based on their findings, to help them effect smooth transfer and ensure continuity. Over the years, the advice has become more specific, away from the general suggestions contained in Youngman and Lunzer, towards concrete suggestions targeted at key staff.

These are intended to be applicable to all children, the frame of reference consistent with truly comprehensive integrated education. Specific guidelines that are particularly relevant to children with designated special educational needs can be abstracted from these universal suggestions to ensure not only the desired continuity – over information exchange, written and verbal communication, record-keeping, assessment procedures, and parental involvement – but to effect a precise match between meeting needs in the secondary sphere, compatible with practice in the primary sphere.

The HMI publication *The Curriculum from 5–16* (DES, 1985) points out that, on the whole, 'schools have been more successful at these transfer points in looking after the pastoral welfare of pupils than in achieving curricular continuity' (p. 50). It goes on to remark that continuity of learning may be facilitated in a number of ways. Amongst these are: primary and secondary schools having an appreciation of each other's curriculum aims and objectives, and devising 'effective systems of records' that will include folders of pupils' works. Secondary schools are exhorted to 'try to adopt the exploratory styles of learning which are characteristic of good primary school practice' (p. 50, see HMI, 1989).

Smith (1985), on the basis of his case study focusing on the views of parents, offers a set of guidelines consisting of 21 pointers towards establishing effective working relations between home and school, to ensure successful transition and adjustment to secondary school.

There is available an ACE information sheet, compiled by teachers and parents at a London comprehensive school, which aims to generate discussion on mechanisms for transfer. Specific suggestions are directed at staff in primary and secondary schools, at parents and at pupils themselves.

2. Facilitating transfer through the National Curriculum

The HMI survey *Curriculum Continuity at 11-plus* (HMI, 1989), although based on a survey carried out prior to the introduction of the National Curriculum, nevertheless provides a frame for schools 'to review their arrangements for curriculum continuity' within the new context. From the small-scale survey of ten pairs of primary schools and their associated secondary schools (ten of these in total), which included a follow-up two terms later to the ten secondary schools, HMI found that most had well-developed links and an articulated policy on transfer and continuity. Pastoral continuity and continuity for children with special needs (especially in maths and language it was noted) were found to be good, though curriculum continuity was less effective.

Evidently a core intention of the 1988 Education Reform Act was to build progression and coherence into children's learning, from starting to leaving school. The National Curriculum constitutes a linear progression from 5 to 16 and will promote these pedagogical aims via programmes of study and schemes of work which, as with attainment targets, are cumulative and offer tangible evidence of learning and achievement over a long period of time. Two other major features will also do much to ease transition for pupils themselves and for teachers effecting cross-phase links:

- *record-keeping* Whichever national (results of SATs) and/or local (Learning Profiles, teacher assessment, records of achievement) systems are adopted, they are intended to be cumulative and accessible to teachers, parents and pupils.
- *cross-curricular dimensions and themes* Not only does the concept

of interwoven subject areas become familiar to pupils so that when they reach secondary school they will encounter structures already known to them, but the themes are intended to have longitudinal relevance and impact. The five themes which the National Curriculum Council has identified as 'seeming to most people to be pre-eminent' (NCC, 1990, p. 4) are: economic and industrial understanding; guidance; health education; education for citizenship; environmental education. The document is explicit that these are equally relevant to primary and secondary schools.

(Also see NCC 1989 for guidance on curriculum continuity within schools and across phases.)

CROSSING THE PERIMETERS FROM PRIMARY TO SECONDARY: SUPPORTING CHILDREN WITH SPECIAL EDUCATIONAL NEEDS

As noted above, the HMI survey (HMI, 1989) identified satisfactory practice in links between primary and secondary for children with special needs. This is echoed in another HMI report on provision for pupils with statements of special educational needs:

> Links across school phases were generally very good. There were visits by teachers in both directions to share information, to observe the pupil in an educational setting, and to meet the parents. Arrangements were made for pupils to familiarise themselves with their new class and school. School records transferred with the pupil and could be extremely valuable. (DES, 1990, p. 15, para. 53)

The best-documented (and now, lamentably, out-of-date) examples of developing practice were the cross-phase links being developed in the ILEA until its demise in April 1990. The three major London reports on primary education (Thomas, 1985), on secondary (Hargreaves, 1984) and special (Fish, 1985) all describe the evolution of such contacts, including the development of clusters, which is an idea now being taken up in many LEAs.

John Sayer, in the companion volume on secondary schools in this series, discusses, in chapter 2, arrangements for transfer and for bringing about continuity. He writes, 'whatever local variation may seem most appropriate, a transfer system should cover curricular continuity, expectations and environment, individual needs, records, and, above all, relationships with pupils and parents'.

ENLISTING PARENTAL SUPPORT: SCHOOLS AND THEIR
COMMUNITIES

This reference to parents touches on one of the features of primary/
secondary school transfer arrangements that ought to be central. It has
been a prime theme of this book, spelled out in Chapter 2 and reiterated
in each chapter, that an integral part of meeting children's needs is the
incorporation of parents into all discussions and decision-making.

In previous chapters, a number of key staff were identified, and, in
Chapter 7, the notion of a key worker who could play a central role in
transfer was put forward. Parents form part of the team, as the Case
Study vignettes in Chapter 7 illustrate. By virtue of their unique knowledge of their child, parents have an incomparable facilitating part to
play in ensuring continuity.

Previous chapters (and see Appendix 2 and Appendix 4) outlined
ways in which parents could contribute their own assessment and
review of progress to the learning and behaviour profiles prepared in
primary schools. The child profile, incorporating up-to-date parental
views, could form a core part of a transfer document. Working in
co-operation with primary and secondary staff parents could also play
a part in assisting their children to acclimatise to secondary school.

The goal of parents and teachers alike to reduce any risk of children
retreating into 'marginality' (see Chapter 2 and Wolfendale, 1983)
applies as much at primary stages as it does at secondary stages. A key
way of combating children's anxieties as they enter the seemingly
daunting territory of secondary school includes parents and teachers
alike:

- talking with their children about longer-term hopes, ambitions and
  fears
- helping them formulate some (provisional) life goals
- exploring with them possibilities and options available in secondary
  school and beyond to acquire life-skills and competence in coping
- helping prepare them for eventual adult citizenship.

Such responsibilities cannot remain the province of secondary staff.
In an age when profound changes to the concept of schooling itself are
envisaged, and the advent of technology renders obsolete some long-
cherished practices to do with transmitting knowledge and skills to our
young, teachers in secondary schools need the backing and co-operation of their primary counterparts. Such solidarity could provide a
firm foundation from which to plan to meet children's universal and
unique needs.

REFERENCES

ACE (no date) *Transfer from Primary to Secondary School, Information Sheet*. Advisory Centre for Education, 1B Aberdeen Studios, Highbury Grove, London N5 2EA.

DES (1985) *The Curriculum from 5-16*. Curriculum Matters no. 2 (an HMI series) London: HMSO.

DES (1990) *Provision for Primary-aged Pupils with Statements of Special Educational Needs in Mainstream Schools, January-July 1989*. London: HMSO.

HMI (1989) *Curriculum Continuity at 11-plus, Education Observed*, 10 London: HMSO.

Fish, J. (Chair) (1985) *Educational Opportunities for All?* Report of the Committee reviewing provision to meet special educational needs. London: ILEA.

Galton, M. and Willcocks, J. (1984) *Moving from the Primary Classroom*. London: Routledge & Kegan Paul.

Hargreaves, D. (Chair) (1984) *Improving Secondary Schools*. Report of the Committee on the curriculum and organisation of secondary schools. London: ILEA.

Measor, L. and Woods, P. (1984) *Changing Schools*. Milton Keynes: Open University Press.

NCC (1989) *Guidance No. 1: A Framework for the Primary Curriculum*. York: National Curriculum Council.

NCC (1990) *Guidance No. 3: The Whole Curriculum*. York: NCC.

Nisbet, J. D. and Entwhistle, N. J. (1969) *The Transition to Secondary Schooling*. London: University of London Press.

Smith, J. (1985) *Transferring to Secondary School*. Home and School Publication, 81 Rustlings Road, Sheffield S11 7AB.

Stillman, A. and Maychall, K. (1984) *School to School*. Windsor: NFER-Nelson.

Taylor, M. and Garson, Y. (1982) *Schooling in the Middle Years*. Stoke-on-Trent: Trentham Books.

Thomas, N. (Chair) (1985) *Improving Primary Schools*. Report of the Committee on primary education. London: ILEA.

Wolfendale, S. (1983) *Parental Participation in Children's Development and Education*. London: Gordon & Breach.

Youngman, M. B. and Lunzer, E. A. (1977) *Adjustment to Secondary Schooling*. Nottingham: Nottingham University School of Education.

Appendices

Appendix 1
Learning profile and profile analysis

PROFILE ANALYSIS OF KENNY, AGED 9 YEARS 8 MONTHS,
REFERRED FOR 'FAILURE TO LEARN' AND 'IMMATURITY'
(23.11.83)

Specific difficulties with learning and behaviour

Teacher   Sees him as not interested and not making progress
               with reading and number.

Parents   See him as switched off reading, interested in
               tables.

EP   Does not know letter sounds, cannot synthesise
               when given sounds, appears lethargic and switched
               off school.

Positive features of learning and behaviour

Father   Kenny works hard at tables at home with him and
               builds intricate models.

EP   Likes drawing, is good at it and enjoyed the
               WISC-R performance tests and then opened up and
               began to chat.

Learning and behaviour needs

At home   Comics, newspaper stories to hear about and dis-
               cuss. Home reading scheme: 5–10 mins only, no
               comment on failures and praise for success.

School   'Tell-a-story' style approach to reading (thorough
               grounding in story so that he can predict what is
               coming, was above average on sequencing sub-
               test). Teacher to show an interest in drawing and
               model-making skills.

Baseline measures Neale reading age 6:0, comprehension age 6:8

Trends (2.3.83)

At school	Lively, enjoys reading own book.
Teacher	Interested in reading for meaning approach.
Problems	Kenny very apprehensive about the second Neale test.
	Teacher leaving at Easter. HT wants Kenny to go to Opportunity class.
Further action	Find out if hearing test done and results.
	Discuss Kenny with new teacher.
	Phone parents with feedback of current situation.

Outcomes (6.7.83)

New teacher	Pleased with Kenny's hard work and effort.
Hearing	Test done, no problem evident at that time.
Parents	Adamant that Kenny go to Opportunity class as he is still making very slow progress with reading and number work, afraid that he will become a behaviour problem at secondary school, like a cousin, if he cannot cope with reading.

NOTES ACCOMPANYING THE USE OF PROFILE ANALYSIS

To be used for children for whom a programme of intervention has been introduced. It fulfils several functions, and its purpose is described below.

1. It is an overall summary of the child's progress. In this instance it complements and supplements the daily or weekly written records that are features of an objectives-based approach (see 8 below). It aims to provide an all-round picture to supplement specific curriculum-based recording or records used for a behavioural programme.
2. It can be used in conjunction with the (pre-test or pre-programme) initial assessment, but is specifically designed to record *continuing* progress through a programme, and to point to trends in the child's learning behaviour.
3. Hence it provides a temporal perspective that could be an additional aid in enabling the programme planners (psychologist, teacher) to reappraise the content and form, and future direction of the programme.
4. It allows for a balanced appraisal of the child's skills and

attainment to be made in that the 'positive' as well as 'negative' aspects of competence are recorded. There is much professional exhortation to assess children's strengths and weaknesses; in fact there are fewer assessment techniques that bring out the learning/behaviour strengths than emphasise the weaknesses, such that it is not surprising that the deficit model is a tempting one to invoke.

5. The profile analysis approach allows all aspects of competence to be appraised; for it is not an assessment tool, rather it is a conceptualisation of functioning that transcends the recording of specific aspects of performance, whilst drawing on such detailed records as a basis for broader conceptualising to be made.

6. The temporal perspective referred to in 3 can be achieved by positing four dimensions:

   (i) *Specific difficulties with learning/behaviour* These will already have been assessed, and used as the basis for planning intervention. Progress measures will be gauged as the difference between pre-programme learning/behaviour and funtioning at the end of the programme. However, these pre- and post-test requirements do not preclude an 'on the spot' estimation during or towards the end of a programme.

   (ii) *Positive features of learning/behaviour* Because a learning/behaviour difficulty is usually the focus of attention, aspects or potential aspects of learning or behaviour that are constructive and could be used to promote overall effective performance are often overlooked. Using this dimension it is possible to draw attention to and record these as evidently present features and also to utilise them in the future.

   (iii) *Learning/behaviour needs* As with (i) these will have been gauged during the initial assessment; however, as the programme proceeds, learning needs may change. Also, a child's motivation, responsiveness and style of learning can alter as a function of the programme (content and teaching method). An additional point to note is that features of learning may only become apparent once a programme is under way, i.e. prior observation and assessment can only reveal a finite amount of information.

   (iv) *Trends* This dimension allows for a transverse appraisal to be made, whereby past and present performance and needs are combined, to effect the making of a prognostic-predictive analysis. In this section the desired/necessary conditions for learning/behaviour can be enumerated as the context or setting for what is perceived to be the likely course of the child's future progress.

7. The profile analysis obtained for any given child can be used, in conjunction with other types of assessment, outcome measures, etc. as a basis for future curriculum planning. One valuable function this approach could serve is to form part of the statementing and review procedures demanded by the 1981 Education Act.

8. The purpose of the profile analysis approach to recording progress differs from that of record-keeping and charting as used in behavioural objectives and precision-teaching approaches (see 1). Often with a highly sequential, very precise curriculum-focused programme, the recording is concerned solely and justifiably with the evident behaviour and measurable progress.

9. A profile analysis approach allows for a modicum of analysis based on inference and extrapolation from manifest behaviour, whilst still insisting on rigorously objective use of terms. The statements should be descriptive, impartial and illuminative in terms of summarising present performance and predicting future functioning. Value judgements play no part in this process; therefore the use of a profile analysis approach is a rigorous conceptual exercise.

   Only terms and categories should be invoked that can be operationally defined, but the design is such that there is leeway and scope for the breadth and depth of professional experience to be utilised.

10. *Background and example*
    The idea of this approach to profile analysis was piloted as part of an intervention project carried out in 1979 (Wolfendale and Bryans, 1980). Quantitative and qualitative pre- and post-test measures were used; measurable gains by the children were recorded. The following examples of the profile analysis of two of the children (JC and SK) convey an impression as to the use of the approach.

The wealth of qualitative data from these forms of illuminative evaluation, sampling a wide range of the children's functioning in conjunction with the standardised test results, enabled us to:

- assess rates of change in performance and progress of the children over the period of time;
- construct comprehensive diagnostic–prognostic profile analyses

for each of the children that could be used as a basis for curriculum planning.

Pre- and post-comparison of the checklists and observation sheets as well as the trend apparent in the teacher's daily records reveal demonstrable progress made by the children in receptive and expressive language skills, perceptual/motor functioning, learning style, and in spontaneous participation in small group work. The teacher also confirmed that all the children were more settled and responsive in the classroom.

The profile analyses given below as examples, in abbreviated form, of two of the six children illustrate the temporal perspective of the programme as well as the children's progress and development through it. The children's functioning is conceptualised along four dimensions; specific difficulties with learning, positive features of learning, learning needs and trends.

Child JC
Specific difficulties with learning. Lethargic; attentive in short bursts; easily distracted by extraneous happenings; 'shy' and reticent in expressive activities like mime; erratic oral contribution.

Positive features of learning. Can retain information over time, *viz.* story time and Kim's game; can participate in written and oral work with interest; shows evident enjoyment when he comprehends and can cope with the task; in paper and pencil tasks can progress when he takes care; good recall.

Learning needs. Needs training to listen consistently over a period of time; needs training to maintain incentive and application; needs help with sequences of information in description or story making; needs repetition of instruction and basic routines.

Trends. Improvement in last few weeks of the programme in attention; sustained involvement and quality of output. His main problems are erratic attention, easy distractibility, and a tendency towards lethargy. Potentially he is keen, interested, responsive, and delighted at signs of his own success.

Child SK
Specific difficulties with learning. Expressive difficulties, cannot explain or describe; inconsistent listening, 'forgets'; erratic, unpredictable immediate memory and recall; left–right difficulties; rushed

learning style in pencil and paper tasks, cannot be over-loaded with too much information.

Positive features of learning.   Can be quick and effective at visual association and shape-copying; can perform hand-eye tasks and miming sequences, although responds unpredictably in these; can be observant.

Learning needs.   Needs reiteration of instructions throughout a task; needs guidance in constructing sentences to explain or describe; needs training in directionality; needs practice with listening and expressive processes to develop immediate and short-term memory.

Trends.   Erratic learning remains; potential interest more evident than before but early 'switch-off' is still apparent; seems aware of his inadequacy; failure is being reinforced by his own performance and other success in the group; potentially responsive.

REFERENCE

Wolfendale, S. and Bryans, T. (1980) Interviewing with learning in the infant school. *Remedial Education* 15 (1).

Appendix 2
Notes for parents: writing a parental profile and reporting on 'My Child at Home'

1. *Introduction* Some parents have had experience of working with and alongside the professionals who teach or look after their children. They have become familiar with completing developmental checklists on their children, reporting upon their children's progress, and having the opportunity to air and share their concerns about their children. These parents have demonstrated how they can effectively match their own knowledge about and insights into their children with the expert knowledge and findings of professional child workers; it is a demonstration of 'equivalent expertise' of each participant in such co-operative ventures.

2. *Contributing to assessment* Parents are *assessing* their children constantly. They *observe* their behaviour, their moods, their worries, their likes and dislikes, their eating habits, sleeping patterns, friendships.

Parents can very often *predict* their children's reactions to people, and events, and can have a good and accurate guess at how their children will behave in a given situation.

Parents can *describe* their children to others, to their friends, and relatives, but also, accurately, to doctors, teachers, and to other people who work with their children.

Parents, with their intimate knowledge of their children, are in the best position to *report* upon their children's behaviour and progress, and to *record*, in writing, as well as orally, and face-to-face, their views, feelings and concerns.

Parents' written accounts of their children can therefore complement teachers' and psychologists' reports and the reports of others who work with children, for example, nursery staff, speech therapists, health visitors, social workers, community workers – and others.

3. *Ways of reporting* This is just a brief list of ways in which parents, working alongside professionals, can observe and record, over a period of days or weeks, their child's behaviour and progress, preferably with other family members, including the child him or herself, if this is possible.

(i) *Keeping a diary*

This might be a brief daily account of behaviour noting important or significant events, and building up a picture over time of when things happen, how you respond, what concerns you.

(ii) *Keeping an observation chart*

You (with professional help if necessary) could devise a way of recording particular behaviour so that you can see, at a glance, after a few days, or weeks, the pattern of behaviour, what happened before, during and after particular incidents, how you all responded.

These ways (i) and (ii) will also help parents to decide how concerned they are about their child at any given time, how seriously to take any matter, and whether or not to take further action.

(iii) *Developmental checklists*

By ticking or answering yes/no to questions or statements about a child's development in, for example, language, self-help skills, social behaviour, a picture can be built up as to how a child is progressing in each and all these areas.

(iv) *Writing a parental profile on 'My Child at Home'*

Putting together on paper your observations, thoughts and feelings about your child will give you an opportunity to comment on his or her development up to the present, and provide you and any professional with a full and rounded picture or profile of behaviour. Any concerns you may have can be included – but this method also gives parents the opportunity to report upon happy, positive aspects of their children and family life as well.

This information is going to be of vital importance to professionals who see children in out-of-home settings (playgroups, nurseries, schools, units, clinics) since children can behave so differently in different situations.

Until recently, it has not been usual for parents and professionals to exchange information on what children are like in different situations, how they behave in different circumstances, what they are good at in school, at home, and in other places.

Decisions as to how children's educational needs can best be met can now be based on an accurate and up-to-date assessment by parents as well as by professionals.

4. *A checklist of pointers* Here is a list of questions to help you to set about constructing a parental profile of your child at home.

- what would you like professionals (teachers, psychologists, and others) to learn about your child at home?
- what information can you give them that they do not already know?
- how best can you describe the positive, good features of your child at home?
- how can you most accurately describe features of behaviour and development of your child at home that concern you?
- what is the most useful way (useful to you and professionals) of summarising your feelings, your concerns, and your views on the situation, and what you feel would be best for your child?
- can you convey in your profile what your child's own views are on his or her situation?

Finally, a look at the future. It is often necessary for a professional to carry out another test or assessment of a child at a later date, to help estimate whether or not progress in development, learning, behaviour has taken place. To have a parental profile available that can be compared with a later one would be an invaluable part of continuing assessment for everyone, and would, without any doubt, be a really helpful contribution to reviewing a child's progress and for deciding how best his or her educational needs can be met.

Appendix 3
Self-reporting by children

EXAMPLE 1:

THE WAY I AM

Name ....   Date ....
Age ....   School ....

What this scale is about

This is a way of helping you to find out more about what you feel and
think about yourself, and to help you decide what are your strong and
your weak points. Also, there may be things you would like to change
in yourself and this scale may help you to decide whether you want to
change any of your behaviour and feelings. Completing this scale
could start you thinking. Be honest – that's the first way in which you
can help yourself.

How to use this scale

The scale consists of a list of feelings and their opposites. The idea is
that you put a tick ($\sqrt{}$) on the line between two feelings where it seems
to be nearest to the way you think you are. The black dot in the middle
of each line is the middle point and it can help you to decide where you
want to put your tick. It might be helpful to you to remember that your
feelings and opinions about yourself will range from

always   mostly   sometimes   sometimes   mostly   always
_____•_____
                         not sure
                         don't know

Here are four examples to show you how the scale works.

Example 1

No. 1

friendly ✓____ unfriendly

Billy sees himself as *always* friendly. He is pleased to find this out about himself.

Example 2

No. 18

reliable ___✓ unreliable

Janet sees herself as *mostly* unreliable. She would like to change and this scale is useful to help her to change.

Example 3

No. 34

hard worker __✓ lazy

It was not easy for Tom to admit that he is *sometimes* lazy and doesn't work hard at school. He wonders how to change.

Example 4

No. 9

popular __✓ unpopular

Linda thinks that she is *sometimes* popular and would like to become more popular. Perhaps she could think about what to do.

The scale

1. Friendly	——————•——————	Unfriendly
2. Honest	——————•——————	Dishonest
3. Tidy	——————•——————	Untidy
4. Sure	——————•——————	Unsure
5. Lucky	——————•——————	Unlucky
6. Happy	——————•——————	Unhappy
7. Fair	——————•——————	Unfair
8. Quiet	——————•——————	Noisy
9. Popular	——————•——————	Unpopular
10. Kind	——————•——————	Unkind
11. Unselfish	——————•——————	Selfish
12. Cheerful	——————•——————	Sad
13. Generous	——————•——————	Mean
14. Good	——————•——————	Bad
15. Successful	——————•——————	Unsuccessful
16. Clean	——————•——————	Dirty
17. Serious	——————•——————	Joking
18. Reliable	——————•——————	Unreliable
19. Relaxed	——————•——————	Tense
20. Patient	——————•——————	Impatient
21. Helpful	——————•——————	Unhelpful
22. Colourful	——————•——————	Drab
23. Obedient	——————•——————	Disobedient
24. Gentle	——————•——————	Aggressive
25. Careful	——————•——————	Careless
26. Confident	——————•——————	Unconfident
27. Lively	——————•——————	Tired
28. Clever	——————•——————	Dull
29. Polite	——————•——————	Rude
30. Strong	——————•——————	Weak
31. Truthful	——————•——————	Untruthful
32. Sensible	——————•——————	Silly
33. Liked	——————•——————	Disliked
34. Hard worker	——————•——————	Lazy
35. Predictable	——————•——————	Unpredictable
36. Risk-taker	——————•——————	Cautious
37. Leader	——————•——————	Easily led
38. Ambitious	——————•——————	Not ambitious

HOW WE WORK

Please tick a YES or NO for each statement.

	YES	NO

THIS SHEET IS ENTIRELY FOR YOU YOURSELF –
TO HELP YOU TO REALISE HOW YOU ARE
GETTING ON IN YOUR SCHOOL WORK

1. I enjoy doing tests.
2. I always sit at the back of the class where the teacher won't see me.
3. Teachers always say that I must work harder.
4. I never seem to have my books.
5. I like answering questions in class.
6. I look out of the window a lot of the time.
7. I ask the teacher for help if I don't understand.
8. Most lessons are boring.
9. Often I start thinking about other things in class.
10. I always try to get better marks in a test than I did before.
11. I try to make my friends talk to me in class.
12. I take a pride in neat work.
13. I get away with things in class.
14. I forget what the teacher tells me to do.
15. I can't find the time to do my homework properly.
16. I worry about tests.
17. Other boys and girls seem to get me into trouble.
18. I check that I have the right books, pens, pencils, rubber, etc.,
    (a) before coming to school
    (b) before going to class.
19. I plan my homework a week ahead.
20. I seem to lose a lot of things.
21. I look up the meaning of words I don't understand.
22. I read in my spare time at home.
23. I talk to others about what I have learnt in school.
24. I look back over my work to make sure that it is my best.
25. I only work when the teacher tells me to.
26. When I am in difficulties I ask for help.
27. When I get poor marks I sit down and work out how to improve.
28. My work is spoiled by careless mistakes.
29. If I miss work through absence I try to copy up the notes.
30. I sometimes find reading books in class difficult.

NOW PUT A STAR * BY ANY OF THESE STATEMENTS THAT YOU FEEL ARE
PARTICULARLY IMPORTANT TO YOU. THEN WRITE ANY ADVICE YOU WOULD
GIVE YOURSELF THAT COULD HELP YOU TO GET ON BETTER WITH YOUR
SCHOOL WORK.

My advice to myself:...
....
....
....
....
....

Name ....   Date ....
School ....

Appendix 4
'Equivalent expertise': a model for parent–professional partnership in assessment

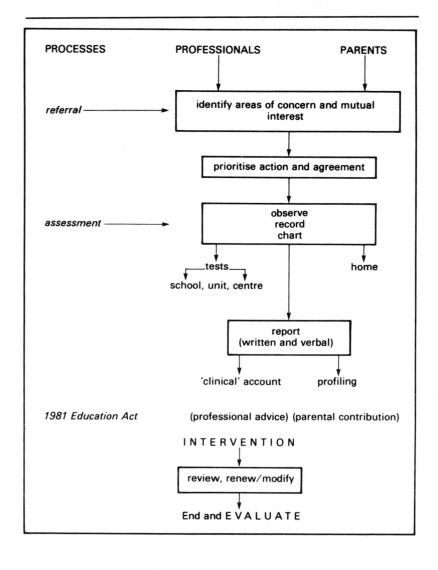

The flow chart outlines the process of parental involvement in assessment within a context of 'equivalent expertise' (Wolfendale, 1983). It can be seen that the Education Act 1981 assessment procedures are fully compatible with this model that can embrace pre- and post-referral co-operation.

REFERENCE

Wolfendale, S. (1983) *Parental Participation in Children's Development and Education*. London: Gordon & Breach.

Appendix 5
Ecological intervention and the technique of eco-mapping

Bronfenbrenner (1979) viewed 'ecological intervention' as a way of analysing children's situations. On the basis of such analysis, their situations could be altered and modified. This whole appraisal perceives the child as central in an ecosystem (ecological system). An ecosystem can be drawn up for each child via the technique of conceptual or eco-mapping, that is, schematic representation that enables close as well as distant influences that impinge upon a child to be plotted in relation to their significance. So a diagram can illustrate where and how any child is juxtaposed in relation to school, family, parents' work, friends, the locality, and places visited. In drawing up an eco-map for one child it is possible to represent significant people, for example, parents, siblings, relatives; teachers, social workers, doctors; peers, friends; shopkeepers, youth leaders, and so on.

This representation can also be done retrospectively, to chart significant people and events from the past, in order to consolidate a picture of major past and present influences.

Constructing an eco-system on behalf of children by means of eco-mapping could be a practical and useful tool. As one technique in the assessment and intervention armoury eco-mapping could serve eight purposes – five general and three more specific:

1. Eco-mapping enables one or more children to be perceived and assessed in relation to a whole class, a year group, a whole school.
2. It enables in and out of school perspectives to be brought together in one eco-map or series of connecting eco-maps.
3. Eco-mapping facilitates and encourages the direct involvement of children and parents in constructing eco-maps, so that what they report and describe first-hand in terms of significant events, places, people is represented on paper.

4. Eco-mapping can be a vehicle for further in-depth exploration of situations, life-events, people, depicted schematically.
5. Information elicited by eco-mapping can be a basis for jointly agreed action.

These are general purposes for using eco-maps; the ones that follow are specific examples.

6. Eco-mapping exercises can be consistent with applied behavioural analyses or other theoretical frameworks for describing and analysing behaviour since it aims to represent significant influences as reported or perceived (by a child or adult) without interpretation. Therefore, if, for example, *Child A* reports a friendship with *Child B*, this can be represented thus in a class-friendship ecomap:

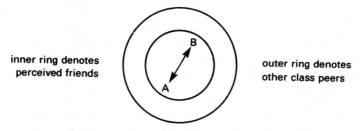

inner ring denotes
perceived friends

outer ring denotes
other class peers

The friendship is neither confirmed, denied, nor explained, merely reported and recorded at this stage. Further analysis can follow.

7. An eco-map is flexible in what it represents and how this representation is made. For example, school can be shown as overlapping with home if, in the child's and adult's view, there is congruence between home and school thus:

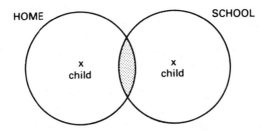

HOME

SCHOOL

x
child

x
child

In the interface between home and school shown above, the parent might be a school governor (this would be marked in some way), or the

parents might be working with the teacher on a home-reading programme (this, too, would be recorded in some way). Another example
demonstrated how size and shapes of eco-maps can confirm the relative importance of people and places in a child's life, *viz*.

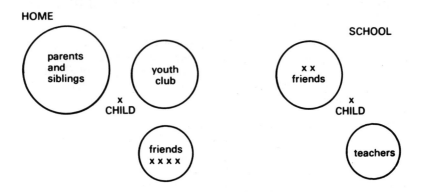

Within the map boundaries, as much detail as is necessary to elaborate
and accurately represent the influencing forces in a child's life can be
given. The example shown above selectively carries little detail, but
further eco-maps can be constructed to magnify and portray influences,
people, etc. For example, the *HOME* eco-map shown above with
minimal detail can itself generate further eco-maps – like an amoeba!
So an eco-map can show what forces impinge and impact upon children and evinces to some extent the multidimensional processes
inherent in all interaction. Arrows can be used to denote particular
relationships and to emphasise how active or dynamic any such interaction is, *viz*:

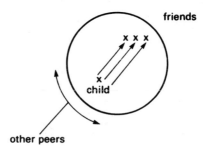

Example A Eco-map of friendship patterns in a classroom

Alternatively, closeness can be represented by concentric circles:

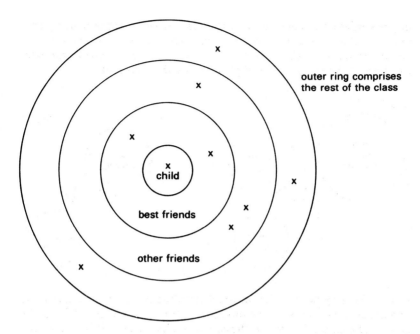

outer ring comprises
the rest of the class

child

best friends

other friends

Example B Eco-map of friendship patterns in a classroom

8. An eco-map can be used as a measure of change. That is, one can
   be drawn up at the outset of investigating a child's situation and
   again at later points in intervention, or simply, at another point
   in the child's life.

The potential of eco-mapping and eco-systems as part of overall assessment and intervention approaches has been described at some length
because their application could provide further valuable tools in
planning and managing for children's learning and other needs in
primary schools. Their value could lie in the fact that these techniques
provide a bridge between individual assessment (see Chapters 3 and 4)
and 'whole-school', or systems, assessment, such that children's needs
are revealed in juxtaposition with school's provision and contribution
of home and the community. Also, as has been stressed, an eco-system
approach is amenable to teamwork.

Ward *et al.* (1986) describe the applications of eco-mapping or constructing 'life maps' with a group of children aged between 11 and 15
years, who had been identified as needing help in relating to past events
in their lives. They were all in residential or foster homes. Since it was
felt that children in care often have poor expressive skills, methods of
communication were used to encourage self-expression, such as drama
and role play, games, and eco-maps. The group members indicated

who and what was important to them, using colours to denote how important in their lives were their parents, other family members, pets, and so on. Ward and his colleagues also introduced the related idea of helping the children to use flow chart reconstructions of their lives as they remembered them.

This work has its origins in earlier psychological exploration into topology, concepts of life space, and, of course, has links with sociometry. Readers wishing to explore further the theory and principles underlying ecological approaches are referred to Bronfenbrenner (1979) and to Apter (1982) for expositions on applications of ecological principle to assessment and intervention within education.

REFERENCES

Apter, S. (1982) *Troubled Children, Troubled Systems*. Oxford: Pergamon Press.

Bronfenbrenner, U. (1979) *The Ecology of Human Development, Experiments by Nature and Design*. Cambridge, MA: Harvard University Press.

Ward, S., Crawley, J., Hughes, J., Martin, N. and Marsland, A. (1986) Playing Apollo. *Community Care* (30 October), 15–17.

Name index

Subject index